Hazlitt Alva Cuppy

The Rise of the Anglo-Indian Empire

Hazlitt Alva Cuppy

The Rise of the Anglo-Indian Empire

ISBN/EAN: 9783744708371

Printed in Europe, USA, Canada, Australia, Japan

Cover: Foto ©ninafisch / pixelio.de

More available books at **www.hansebooks.com**

THE
RISE OF THE ANGLO-INDIAN EMPIRE.

DER

PHILOSOPHISCHEN FACULTÄT DER UNIVERSITAT

HEIDELBERG

ALS PROMOTIONSSCHRIFT VORGELEGT

HAZLITT ALVA CUPPY.

THE
Rise of the Anglo=Indian Empire.

BY

HAZLITT ALVA CUPPY.

Heidelberg, June 1892.

PREFACE.

I wish to acknowledge the kindness of those connected with the Library and Record Department of the India Office. The favors shown by those connected with the British Museum are well-known to every scholar who has had the opportunity of research at that place.

I found the Records in the India Office in a very unsatisfactory condition. Every effort is being made to sort out, classify and arrange the great piles of manuscript, the contents of which no one as yet knows. Considerable progress has already been made, and the Records thus arranged have been used as far as conditions would allow.

The best work on the subject of this sketch is Mill's "British India." Another able work is "The British in India," by the Right Hon. Sir William M. James, Lord Justice of Appeal. I have also consulted many other works, among them Sir William Hunter's "Gazetteer of India," J. Talboys Wheeler's "Early Records of British India (1879)," and his "Madras in the Olden Times," Murray's "History of British India," Nolan's "History of British India," Macfarlane's "History of British India," "Diary of William Hedges," "Pepys' Diary," Macpherson's "Annals of Commerce," Anderson's "History of Commerce," "Macaulay's Essays," the various histories of England, etc.

H. A. CUPPY.

HEIDELBERG, VILLA FELSECK.
 June 8th, 1892.

CONTENTS.

PART I.

			PAGE.
CHAPTER	I.	INTRODUCTION	7
,,	II.	ENGLAND AT THE END OF THE 16TH CENTURY	10
,,	III.	INDIA AT THE END OF THE 16TH CENTURY	13
,,	IV.	LEADING UP TO THE EAST INDIA COMPANY	20
,,	V.	THE COMPANY ORGANIZED	27
,,	VI.	UP TO THE MASSACRE OF AMBOYNA	33
,,	VII.	INCLUDING ACCOUNT OF MASSACRE OF AMBOYNA AND EVENTS UP TO CHARTER GRANTED BY CHARLES II.	41
,,	VIII.	UP TO THE UNION OF THE TWO COMPANIES	51
,,	IX.	INCLUDING AN ACCOUNT OF THE GERMAN COMPANIES	59
,,	X.	UP TO THE BATTLE OF PLASSY	65

PART II.

CHAPTER	I.	THE RISE OF DOMINION	75
,,	II.	ON THE WEST COAST	80
,,	III.	PARLIAMENT BEGINS TO ASSUME SOME AUTHORITY IN INDIAN AFFAIRS	84
,,	IV.	WARREN HASTINGS	87
,,	V.	UP TO THE END	91

APPENDIX.

CHAPTER I.

INTRODUCTORY.

WHEN in 1858 by Act of Parliament, the Government of India was taken out of the hands of the East India Company and given over to national control, there were probably few who reflected, that the greatest oligarchy the world has ever known came to an end. Yet it was true.

The Anglo-Indian Empire stands almost without a parallel in history.

From a handful of English speculators in 1599, pleading with their queen for privileges to trade with the East, the sweep of little more than a century shows us a mercantile monopoly, wielding great power and controlling vast wealth, its stockholders drawing ten per cent. on a capital stock of over three millions sterling.

At the middle of the present century, we find the same company the sole political guardian and controller of the teeming millions of India. It has a revenue and army greater than many European states. It has in its two and a half centuries of growth, founded an empire as notable and more lasting than that of Alexander the Great. We shall trace the rise and growth of this empire. We shall see an association of traders establish agencies, which, in the march of events, grow into the capitals of a British empire.

It is not our aim to cover the field in detail. Ours shall be a more modest task, yet one which does not necessarily possess less of interest or practical worth. We hope, however, to introduce into this sketch enough of minuteness of detail to awaken lively sympathy in those characters who were the instigators and builders of the Anglo-Indian Empire, as well as in the chief events of its growth, else our attempt at history will fail of its purpose.

We shall study our subject from itself, rather than from the outside. Yet as our judgment of events is more or less comparative, we must at the same time include in our treatise enough auxiliary facts to give us some sort of a true conception of the period, of its beginnings, and the environments of its growth.

We shall attempt to grasp, as far as lies in our power, those elements which gave it life, and made that life progressive.

We shall avoid such statistics and such Oriental names and expressions as we do not think absolutely necessary to the proper conception of the work in hand. Confine our scope as we may, we shall still find the onward march of the movement started by a few English adventurers, a curious and an interesting study.

The history of the East India Company really begins with that gathering in London, September 23rd, 1600. For some years the more enterprising London merchants had been wrought up to a high pitch over the reputed wealth of the Orient. It had been the chief topic of conversation. In their day-dreams they had built themselves palaces hung about with tapestries set with sparkling gems, brought from their far away land. Had Solomon not drawn his wealth from the Indies? Had not the rich productions of this wonder-land from time immemorial proved a never failing fountain of riches? Whence the brilliancies of the court of Ahasuerus, the gems which lighted up the floating gardens of Babylon, if not from India? The temples to the Olympian gods, the splendors of the courts of the Cæsars, derived their opulence from the same source. And even in their own day Spain and Portugal were boasting their quantities of gold and silver, their countries fragrant with the perfumes from the Orient; nor was this all. Their very door-neighbors, the Dutch, had just returned with—to what extent no one knew—precious cargoes from this land where the direct rays of the sun transformed common earth to gold.*

* Sir William Monson's Theory, in Collection of Voyages and Travels.

English merchants must arouse themselves if they would be participants in, and enjoy the fruits of, this new field of such wondrous resources.

And so they agitated, called assemblies, discussed, planned, disbanded and assembled again. At length, goaded by the desire to delve in this mine of wealth first hand, and smarting with jealousy at the strides of their less ostentatious neighbors, the Dutch, they draw up the following paper and carried it about for signatures:

" The names of suche persones as have writtin with there owne handes to venter in the pretended voiage to the Easte Indias (the whiche it maie please the Lorde to prosper) and the Somes that they will adventure the xxii. September, 1599."* What did it matter about the spelling? The names were added at once, almost every branch of trade being represented.

Then came that gathering in Founders' Hall one year later. Their Queen had been politic and there had been a wearisome delay, " by reason of a treatye of peace in hand between the Queene's Ma'es and the Kinge of Spaine." For this reason she had " denied to geave them suche a warrant, as thinking it more beneficiall for the general state of merchaundize to enterteyne a peace, etc."† Now she had yielded, and it was announced before the assembly that " it was her Ma'es pleasure that they should proceade in their purpose."‡ And their dreams were to become realities.

*From Court Records of East India Company.

†Report of Divers Committees, 16th October, 1599, from Records in India Office.

‡Public Records, India Office.

CHAPTER II.

ENGLAND AT THE END OF THE 16TH CENTURY.

LET him who can, describe adequately that period in the history of the English people, when, awakening from the lethargy which had hung over them during the middle ages, they started into that newer life, with a vigor such as no other people have ever shown. It was as the full sunlight that follows close upon the storm-black clouds. It was as if nature should at one great bound, transform herself from the dark and gloomy buds of winter to the full bloom of summer.

What shall we say of that folk, for the most part leading a life of greatest simplicity, their houses being built of wood and clay with layers of filthy rushes for flooring, their little villages dotting the coast about, being but clusters of mere hovels, in which fishermen lived as their fathers and mothers had lived ever since the time of Edward III.

There was no change, no improvement, no new ambitions. They plied their boats to Bordeaux and Cadiz, and to the Continental ports. They steered north for their annual supply of cod-fish, sailed up and down the channel and around their own coasts.

New explorations possessed no novelty or attraction for them. The farmers tended their flocks, cultivated to a modest extent the necessities of life. The Cornwall miner dug his bit of tin. In Kent and Sussex they worked their iron. Bands of robbers roamed the hills. All held to the traditions of their fathers even more tenaciously than Oxford University did to the thirty-nine articles of its "Ancient Regime."

The country gentleman was satisfied with a wooden house of small pretensions. Its furniture was plain, looking to necessities rather than comfort, and wholly devoid of luxury. London, the great center, was largely a city of small wooden and mud houses, with a population of less than 200,000, including all suburbs. Yet almost at a single bound these hardy, conservative, traditional people break away from the shackles, which have so long held them fast, and electrify us with the thrill of their new life.

The chrysalis once broken, out into this new world issue the latent desires and geniuses of centuries. A Stratford boy finds his way to London and writes plays for all time. A young lawyer about the court of a favorite queen writes the " Novum Organum." An English bard sings from the Irish hills and the " Faerie Queen," is ours. From Plymouth sails the vessel which is the second to circumnavigate the globe. London merchants toss about on their pillows dreaming of the wealth ascribed to the far-away Indies.

The transformation extended to every phase of their civilization. Farms were improved until they produced double their annual yield. Their " rough and wattled farm houses were being superseded by dwellings of brick and stone." They began to use dishes of metal in place of the crude, wooden utensils of their fathers. The amassed wealth of the London merchant was expended in building himself great houses with extravagant wainscoting and figured gables. There were parapeted fronts and glass windows, until Lord Bacon was driven to mutter : " You shall have sometime your houses so full of glass that we cannot tell where to come to be out of the sun or the cold."

Noblemen sought the hand of daughters of these merchant princes for their sons. Greater care and taste were taken in the line of dress. The Queen boasted her " three thousand robes." Every phase of life was permeated by the new regime. " It is," says Green, " from this period indeed, that we can first date the rise of a conception which seems to us now a peculiarly English one, the conception of domestic comfort." Pulsating with the possession of this new energy England presents a panorama of thought, enterprise, imagination and eloquence, which combine to illuminate it with the most dazzling light.*

However much may be said in praise of any period, we must not lose sight of the fact that there is another side, unfortunately not so inviting. With increase of wealth and a taste of luxury, comes increased desire for the same. Consequent dissipations followed. People flocked to London; the nobility strove to mingle about a brilliant court. Coffee-houses were filled with players, playwrights, poets and every variety of literary aspirants, who drank and drank again, until their brain as well as their legs refused longer to serve them.

The proverbial thrift vanished from the land; men speculated, and "young bloods" gambled away fortunes at a single sitting.

"England," said Cecil, "spendeth more on wines in one year than it did in ancient times in four years."

At the court ruled a queen who was the idol of her people, yet she was a coquette, the subject of scandals, who could speak a lie as easily as the truth if it only answered her purpose as well. Fond of show, of velvets, silks, pearls and diamonds—and handsome men. Loud, with a masculine voice, stubborn, passionate, easily provoked to anger, profane sometimes, petulant, coarse, avaricious. She not only applauds and rewards piracy, but gives it royal sanction and encouragement by investing her private funds and reaping some of the illegal benefits. And yet Elizabeth combined in her make-up such virtues as made her beloved by her people and as will make her name revered through all time. We shall have occasion to refer to these in a subsequent chapter.

* "There never was, anywhere, anything like the sixty or seventy years that elapsed from the middle of Elizabeth's reign to the Restoration. In point of real force and originality of genius, neither the age of Pericles, nor the age of Augustus, nor the times of Leo the Tenth, or of Louis the Fourteenth, can come at all into comparison. For in that short period, we shall find the names of almost all the very great men that this nation has ever produced; the names of Shakspere and Bacon, and Spenser, and Sidney, of Raleigh, . . . men, all of them, not merely of great talents and accomplishments, but of vast compass and reach of understanding, and of minds truly creative and original."—Lord Jeffrey, in *Edinburgh Review*, Vol. II.

CHAPTER III.

India at the End of the 16th Century.

To attempt to give anything in the way of Indian history is without the pale of our present purpose. But something about the people with whom we shall have to do is essential.

When we transport ourselves to India we find quite another country from what the western world then thought. It was not a land flowing with milk and honey. It was not dotted about by country palaces hung with fine tapestries or spread with luxurious rugs. Its inhabitants did not continually bask in the aroma of fragrant and delicious odors. Its prairies were not set with diamonds and precious stones, nor were there the scenes of great fields of golden grain made merry by the songs of happy harvesters. No nuggets of gold or silver were washed down from the mountains and left lying about the plains through which the waters of the sluggish rivers found their way to the sea.

And yet no other country on the globe has been so richly endowed by nature. It possesses almost every diversity of climate, from the scorching heat of the tropics to the barren cold of the Himalaya slopes forming its north-east boundary. To the south like a hugh wedge India has pushed her way into the sea, and the waves play upon the larger part of her frontier. From almost impenetrable jungles, where nature runs riot in unbounded luxuriance, through which the waters of her many rivers are scarce able to find their way, the varying degrees of elevation produce the different shades of climate and degrees of productiveness which are usually common to a much greater extent of country. As we take a cursory glance at India during the latter half of the 16th century and study the conditions, manners and modes of her people, we find those elements in her civilization which compel the thought to break over the bounds of this century, and give itself over to surveying, weighing and comparing the progress of all peoples in all ages. Enough that it suggests the thought. Ours is to do with what we find—but does not what we find connect us inseparably with the past centuries? As we mingle with these Hindoos with their slender though well built frame, look into their dusky faces, or listen to the ring of their conversation, are we not in some measure familiarizing ourselves with the Persians and Egyptians of the time of Alexander—may we not say, with the Chaldeans and Babylonians of the time of Cyrus? Yes, for century after century rolls by and leaves in this part of the earth scarce any perceptible improvement. Through all the centuries of her history one seeks in vain for successive steps of progress marking either age or century.* True "Darius subdued the Indians" as Herodotus says, and Alexander carried his victorious arms beyond the Indus; but if the Greek sway of nearly a century and a half was productive of anything progressive, it was swept away by the conquering hordes of the barbarians pouring irresistible, down from Central Asia. During the first quarter of the 11th century, Mohmood, a Persian ruler whose father had risen from a Greek slave, invaded India not less than thirteen times, setting up on that side of the Indus the thrones of the Mahomedans.

The middle of the 13th century is significant as being the time of the first invasion of the Moguls, destined to play so important a part in the subsequent history of the empire. The end of the 14th century Tamerlane carried his banners beyond Delhi. The first half of the 16th century witnesses

---

* "From the scattered hints contained in the writing of the Greeks, the conclusion has been drawn that the Hindus, at the time of Alexander's invasion, were in a state of manners, society and knowledge, exactly the same with that in which they were discovered by the nations of modern Europe : nor is there any reason for contradicting this opinion."— Mill's British India, Vol. I., Book II., Chapter I., p. 101.

the founding of the Great Mogul dynasty. At the time of which we speak Akbar was on the throne, which he had ascended when scarce fourteen years old (1556). But his young life had been one of difficulties and misfortune. If we accept the authority of our best evidence Akbar was one of the great monarchs of India. He was brave, full of daring and heroism. Conquering more by the influence of his bold personality than by the number of his forces, he very soon so wrought upon the minds of his Oriental subjects that they ascribed to him marvellous wondrous works and the power of the mysterious and preternatural. The Catholic missionaries from Goa, who, at his request, spent some time at his court, describe him as being a man of fair countenance, strongly intellectual, keen concerning anything new and strange. He was proud of the hero worship of his subjects, presenting himself mornings in full view of the multitudes, who prostrated themselves to the earth before him. Step by step he extended his sway from the mountains of Persia and Tartary on the one side to within the territory of the southern part of the peninsula—the Deccan—on the other. He is accredited with having been the monarch of fifty millions of subjects, possessing a revenue enjoyed by few princes.*

But what of the government, religion and daily life of the masses of this vast empire. We have said the centuries resulted in little advancement; in just what state of civilization do we at the end of this (the 16th) century find them? Since all our knowledge is more or less comparative, it would be unfair to judge them by any 19th century standard; but we may judge them according to the advantages which the centuries and a bountiful nature have cast at their feet. Weighed in these balances they are found wanting. Their government was an absolute monarchy in its crudest form. The Hindoo legislators never dreamed of anything other than the one man power, although thrones were constantly usurped

* "In revenue the Emperor doubtless exceeds either Turk or Persian, or any eastern prince; the sums I dare not name, but the reason. All land is his, no man has a foot."—Sir Thomas Roe to Archbishop of Canterbury.

by the strongest man the subjects as constantly paid their allegiance to the man in power.* Whoever was able to place himself on the throne was absolute over all. In order to govern his possessions he must divide them into provinces, placing a viceroy over each, who exerted the same unlimited power over his own territory as the king did over all. These vicegerents ranked from lords over one town to rulers over one thousand towns. The expenses of each were paid from his own revenues and the balance remitted to his over lord, and passed thus along until some fraction of it at length came to the royal treasury. Their laws provide for an advisory council, but in such a way as to leave the full power with the ruler. "We may assume it," says Mill, "as a principle in which there is no room for mistake, that a government constituted and circumstanced, as that of the Hindus had only one limit to its exactions, the non-existence of anything further to take."

The only restraints laid upon rulers were those of religion. The priests in their sphere exerted enormous power among the people. Everything was enacted by deity. He was the performer of the most astonishing feats. He inspired the Laws of Menu,† and separated the people into the different castes. Their religion is anything else but indicative of an advanced state of civilization. What must we say of that fanaticism which extols acts of self-mutilation too horrible to repeat in print, that encourages self-murder in various

* "A King is formed of particles from the chief guardian deities, and consequently surpasses all mortals in glory. Like the sun, he burns eyes and hearts; nor can any human creature on earth gaze on him. He, fire and air; He, the god of criminal justice; He, the genius of wealth; He, the regent of waters; He, the lord of the firmament. A King even though a child must not be treated lightly from an idea that he is a mere mortal; no, he is a powerful divinity who appears in human shape."—"Laws of Menu," Chapter VII. (Quoted by Mill).

† Gibbon, Chapter I., p. 269, speaking of the Koran says: "An endless, incoherent rhapsody of fable, and precept, and declamation which seldom excites a sentiment or an idea, which sometimes crawls in the dust and is sometimes lost in the clouds." ",Yet," says Mill, "it is a superior composition to any work among the Hindus."

forms, from drowning in the Ganges to that of slow tortures until the soul is supposed to leave the body and merge into the supreme, that leads the wife to lie beside the corpse of her husband on the funeral pile and yield, in agony which beggars description, her life to the flames.

It is without our present range to give even the faintest conception of the ritual of the Hindoos, which from the Brahman to the Soudar includes the minutest details covering almost every phase of human life.* It contains details wearisome, vulgar, and absurd. Suffice it to say, there is much that implies depravity, feeds the most absurd superstition and makes its votaries such slaves as does the system of no other people of whom we have record.† The everyday routine of life in India at the end of the 16th century does not lead one to form either a very extravagant idea of its wealth, or of the civilization of its people.

There are one or two very simple exponents of a nation's progress. The condition of the women is one. Woman rises from a condition of abject slavery among a barbarian people to an exalted rank among a cultured people. We need only

---

* Among the religious laws regarding marriage the following is interesting :—

"Let him not marry a girl with reddish hair, nor with any deformed limb, nor one troubled with habitual sickness ; nor one either with no hair or too much, nor one immoderately talkative ; nor one with inflamed eyes ; nor one with the name of a constellation, of a tree, of a river, of a barbarous nation or of a mountain, of a winged creature, a snake or a slave ; nor with any name raising an image of terror. Let him choose for his wife a girl whose form has no defect : who has an agreeable name : who walks gracefully like a phenicopteros, or like a young elephant ; whose hair and teeth are moderate respectively in quantity and size; whose body has exquisite softness."—"Institutions of Menu," Chap. III., pp. 106-109, quoted by Mill, Vol. I., p. 293.

† "We have seen likewise that by the division of the people into castes and the prejudices which the detestable views of the Brahmens raised to separate them, a more degrading and pernicious system of subordination was established among the Hindus, or at any rate the vices of that system were carried to a more destructive height than among any other people. And we have seen that by a system of priestcraft, built upon the most enormous, irrational and tormenting superstition that ever harassed and degraded any portion of mankind, their minds were enchained more intolerably than their bodies."—Mill, Book II., Chapter X., p. 452.

to say in this connection that blunted as must have been the finer feelings and sensibilities of the sex in their present condition, their dependence was such that many an Indian mother murdered her own little girl baby to save it from a life of contempt and humiliation at the hands of the stronger sex. They are usually referred to as "wretches of the most base and vicious inclinations," and "on whose nature no virtuous or useful qualities can be engrafted." "Their husbands should be diligently careful in guarding them: though they well know the disposition with which the lord of creation formed them."*

The condition of the public highways is another indication of a country's advancement. As for their roads, there were none to speak of. At a much later time a Baptist missionary writes: "It is a fact that there is not a road in the country made by the Hindoos, except a few that lead to holy places." At best they had but paths along which the sheep, and men used to transport their articles of traffic, might find their way. Most articles of trade were carried by men to and from the markets. The highest type of wagon was a primitive vehicle made of two wheels sawed from the end of a tree, joined by an ungainly axle.† Their attempts at agriculture were quite as crude, their ploughing being a mere scratching and cross-scratching in the dirt with sharp bits of wood, pulled by their native cattle.

True, they could weave, and spin metaphysical speculations (not always an indication of deep learning), and in many of the arts they had made considerable advance, usually those which were best suited to the nature of the Hindoo.

The Hindoo character is a study in itself. They are in stature below the average European, in build slender and deli-

* "Institutes of Menu."

† "To lessen the friction between the wheel and axis, and save either his wretched cattle, or his own ears, the simple expedient of greasing his wheels never suggested itself to the mind of a rijot of Hindustan."— Mill, Vol I., Book II., Chapter VIII., p. 347.

cate, but well developed, agile, with a keen sense of touch, and acute organs of sensibility; rather fine-featured, gentle and at the same time cruel* and ferocious; timid, yet courageous; cowardly, but facing death as do no other people; lazy, yet capable of enduring more than stronger races. Avaricious, penurious, phlegmatically inactive, treacherous, deceitful, prone to flattery, litigious, quarrelsome, unclean,† arrogant with power but servile to superiors, subtle, false, inhospitable, unsympathetic, yet patient in enduring pain unto death, with little of filial or conjugal affection, the " offspring of a wild and ungoverned imagination ".‡ But with all this an analysis of the Hindoo character will reveal to us the capacity at least of much that is good and noble. It is among these people that our English traders will come, little thinking they are to be the founders of an empire.

* We may cite one example of Indian cruelty so late as 1715. Some 780 Sike prisoners had been captured and rode into the capital of their victorious captors. These accompanying victors carried some two thousand gory heads lifted high on poles. The Sikes were set apart to be killed, one hundred each day, according to Elphinstone, the chief " was exhibited in an iron cage, clad in a robe of cloth, and a scarlet turban : an executioner behind him with a drawn sword ; around him were the heads of his followers on pikes, and even a dead cat was struck on a similar weapon to indicate the extirpation of everything belonging to him. He was then given a dagger and ordered to stab his infant son, and on his refusing the child was butchered before his face, and its heart thrown in his face. He was at last torn in pieces with hot pinchers."

† Their houses were generally of mud. Their village streets were filthy, and the lower classes were nasty as to their person. "Brahmans and religious people plaster the pavement and sometimes the walls with cow dung, and although this act proceeds from a spirit of religion, yet it is of use in keeping out insects."—" Sonnerat Voyages," liv. III., Chap. I., quoted by Mill

"The Bayans (Hindoo merchants) for the most part live in humble cells or sheds, crowding three or four families together into an hovel, with goats, cows, and calves, all chamber fellows, that they are almost poisoned with vermin and nastiness; so stupid that, notwithstanding chints, fleas, and musketoes, torment them every minute, dare not presume to scratch when it itches lest some relation should be untenanted from its miserable abode." Fryer's—" Travels."

‡ " The lower orders in other countries are often lamentably debased : in Hindustan they are degraded infinitely below the brutes."—Mill, Vol. I., p. 287.

CHAPTER IV.

Leading up to the East India Company.

According to Pensionary De Witt* there were no merchants in Europe previous to the tenth century, excepting a few among the Italian Republics, trading with Indian caravans of the Levant. " So that each nation was forced to sow, build, and weave for itself, to the northward and eastward where there were neither foreign nor inland merchants. . . . The Flemings lying nearest to France were the first that began to earn their livings by weaving, and sold the same in that fruitful land."

The commercial centers following this period were the Hanse towns.† Up to the time of Edward III. the limited commerce of England was carried on largely by the agents of this league, Cologne standing at the head of the English branch of their trade. The center of this trade was the Stalhoff (Steelyards) in London, and it was their own boats that carried their products up and down the Thames. After the discovery of America‡ the conquests of Cortez and Pizarro, the rounding of the Cape of Good Hope by Vasco de Gama, Lisbon and Cadiz became great marts of

---

* " Interest of Holland."

† A league of German cities combining for mutual defense and protection. It did not, as we have been accustomed to think, spring full-fledged into existence in 1241; but it was an organization of slow growth, a natural result of the condition of the times.—(See the publications of the Hanes Historical Society.)

‡ There seems to have been a general looking forward to the discovery of a new world. Dante's Vision of Purgatory, alluding to " Southern Cross." Luigi Pulci, b. 1431, d. 1487.
" Men shall descry another hemisphere,
Since to one center all things tend."
Pliny and Seneca hint at another continent.

trade and centers of wealth. Into Cadiz especially came the spices and perfumes of India, the plunder of Mexico and Peru, the gold, silver, and jewels from the newer quarters of a realm which overshadowed that of any other nation. Before the middle of the 16th century Milan, Naples and Sicily, Arragon, Castile and Burgundy, as well as the vast possessions of the new worlds, "clustered on the brow of her sovereigns." Flanders in spite of revolt was under her sway. Philip, notwithstanding his vast possessions, was not a true cosmopolitan. He was thoroughly a Spaniard, living in and ruling from Madrid, his immense domain. He was an indefatigable worker, allowing no man to act as his minister, but going into the minutest details himself. His army was made up of soldiers as brave as the Romans of old, daring, skilful, but cruel. Catholicism was the great common bond. His ambition knew no bounds, but he was slow, cautious and timid to a fault. He was the great opposer of Coligny and the Huguenots. His country was soon to plunge the Germans into the Thirty Years' war. He even planned the subjugation of England. In the meantime Antwerp had become the great commercial center. The Dutch had become the great carriers and distributers from the southern markets to northern Europe. Persecution in France and the Lowlands had driven many of their best tradesmen and artisans to London, where they found a hearty welcome. England awakens, men read with keenest interest the detailed and exaggerated reports of traders. The Londoners recall the attempts made under Edward IV. and Henry VIII. to seek respectively a north-east and a north-west passage to the east. Already were their sailing vessels touching at the Canary islands on the coast of Guinea and Brazil, while fish were brought from the distant shores of Newfoundland. They had already a small trading station at Archangel. A Russian company had sprung up. The Levant Company was organized to secure to the nation the benefits of Oriental trade. Elizabeth's peaceful reign had fostered these new movements. The desire for wealth and luxury took strong hold on the Court itself. William Hawkins (1530) had opened trade with Africa.* Francis Drake had made his tour around the world, returning after nearly three years to be fondled by Royalty. The Queen accepted a part of the plunder of his piracy,† wore the jewels he presented her in her crown and in return made him a knight.‡ Private gentlemen were carried away by this brilliant voyage, many, like Sir Walter Raleigh, investing their whole property in fitting out vessels to emulate the example of the Plymouth sailor. Thomas Cavendish¶ was the second Englishman to circumnavigate the globe and return to his country with most wonderful accounts of Oriental wealth. India was the great topic of conversation; it raged like a fever. Every scrap of information was seized and greedily devoured.‖ In the

* In the famous Naval Gallery in Greenwich hangs an old painting of Drake, Hawkins and Cavendish. It gives us a very good idea of the three great pioneers of English commerce. It represents Drake with high forehead, bold prominent blue eyes, which show gentleness combined with daring. He was of good physique and strong. Hawkins has a somewhat larger head, less prominent eyes, wider forehead, mouth and ears large. His face shows rather keen perceptive faculties. Cavendish was spare in build, smooth-faced except for a light moustache. His face betokens ambition, recklessness combined with boldness and quick determination.

† Monson speaking of Drake's voyage says : " His Design being to steal, and thereby to disturb the Peace of Princes, to rob the poor Traveler, to shed the Blood of the Innocent, and to make Wives Widows and Children fatherless."—Sir W. Monson's Naval Tracts in Collection of Voyages and Travels, Vol. III., p. 400. The old ship was still lying at Deptford when the above was written.

‡ Leaving Plymouth, December 13th, 1577, he passed the Straits of Magellan, followed along the western coast of South America, Mexico and California, taking all the prizes that fell in his way, until his hull was weighed down with gold and silver, passing thence across the Pacific, through the islands of the Orient, where he added to his cargo, finally reaching Plymouth again September 26th, 1580.

¶ He says Cavendish had spent his means at Court and went to regain his fortune by gaining prizes.

‖ It is worth remarking that although Akbar " had bequeathed to his posterity an empire containing more than twenty times the population and yielding more than twenty times the revenue " of England, that the English had absolutely no just conception of India. " It is curious and interesting," says Macaulay (History of England) " to consider how little the

Calendar of State Papers (Vol. XXXI, June, 1589) I find the following remark, which illustrates the passion of the time. " There are adventurers strongly appointed for the Indies gone or going from the West County under the Earl of Cumberland, Chidley and others, to pilfer as Cavendish did." Another writer puts it as follows: " In the same year 1589 the brave and enterprising Earl of Cumberland with several ships sailed in a private adventure to the Azores or Western Isles, where he took many good prizes, etc."*

Queen Elizabeth had come to the throne when wise statesmen were wont to prophesy that England was the certain prey of either France or Spain. But such a fate was not in store for her. Indeed, the very contrary; for she was again to take her place as one of the three great powers of the world, under the banner of this queen; who found time to study her Greek Testament, read the Church Fathers, familiarize herself with the classics, translate, make verses, not poetic perhaps, but harmonies containing some bright thoughts and deep resolves, and write skilful letters " succinct and rich in matter."† She was a good talker, showing off to advantage in conversation when she willed, cherished personal homage and adoration, and by a peculiar combination of grandeur and condescension often awakened it. She was prudent enough to surround herself with good councillors, never letting them know just how much they were in her favor. But she is beset with dangers on every side, her life threatened; religious strife among the people; her ministers thirsting for war. She had to face Spain, France,

two countries, destined to be one day so closely connected, were then known to each other. The most enlightened Englishman looked on India with ignorant admiration. The most enlightened natives of India were scarcely aware that England existed. Our ancestors had a dim notion of endless bazaars, swarming with buyers and sellers, and blazing with cloth of gold, with variegated silks, and with precious stones, of treasuries where diamonds were piled in heaps, etc."

* Anderson's " Origin of Commerce," Vol. II., p. 172.

† I am largely indebted to Ranke's History of England for what immediately follows.

excommunication by the Pope, the Jesuits and the whole Catholic world. Fortunately the jealousies of her neighbors were greatly in her favor. France and Spain were great rivals and hated each other. France pleaded for an alliance by marriage and Elizabeth seemingly encouraged it, petting the homely Duke of Alençon, calling him her pet frog, not wholly unappropriate; for at her bidding he jumped back and forth across the channel or ran over to aid the Netherlands. Once when walking with him in the palace gardens at Greenwich,* followed by two of her nobles, the French ambassador suddenly presented himself and reproached her for constantly putting off the definite decision. For answer she turned and kissed the Duke, saying, "Tell your master he shall be my husband." She kept up her game well, hoodwinking Philip and taking every advantage of his Fabian policy. Thus unhanded, assaulted as she was by all the powers of intrigue and treason, she saved her crown, England and the Protestant cause. As Ranke aptly remarks: "It is surely the greatest happiness that can be granted to any human being while defending his own interests to be defending the interests of all. Then his personal existence expands into a central part of the world's history. There never was, probably, a sovereign who maintained conflicts of so wide importance amid so great dangers and with so great success. Her grandfather had begun a political emancipation from continental influence, her father an ecclesiastical one. She took up and accomplished the work against Rome and Spain, all the while her country developing." "Her memory is inseparably connected with the independence and power of England."† It was when the Queen learned of Philip's proposed invasion, that she sent Sir Francis Drake with a fleet of forty ships to cruise off the Spanish coast. During this successful cruise a number of Portuguese ships were taken. In one of these there were found a number of documents, the contents of which, when made known in

* From Froude's History of England.
† Ranke, p. 355.

London, determined the merchants to arrange for some plan for trading with the East.* Then after the defeat of the Armada (1588), England stood on an equal footing with the other powers. She had in fact become the great sea power. The English " sea dogs " penetrated the farthest seas, and brought into her harbors the fruits of their ill-gotten gains. There was according to Bruce early in 1589 a memorial † presented to the Lords of the Council, which evidently was not looked upon with disfavor, if we may judge from Captain Raymond's voyage in 1591.‡ Notwithstanding the disastrous outcome of this attempt they were not dissuaded from further attempts at trade. Two years later we find the Queen permitting two of her own war ships to join in " with some merchants ships fitted out by Sir Walter Raleigh and commanded by one Sir John Boroughs, Sir Martin Frobisher and Sir Robert Cross. The first took a Biscayner of 600 tons laden with Iron Stoves, etc., for the West Indies; next they forced a great East India Carrack on shore at the Azores, where it was burnt ; soon after they met with the greatest of all the East India Carracks, which they took, though with great slaughter, and carried her into Dartmouth, where she surprised all who saw her, being the largest ship ever seen in England. The cargo, . . . moderately valued at £150,000, was divided amongst the adventurers, of whom the queen was the principal."¶

We must not lose sight of the fact, however, as Monson appropriately puts it, that the English " were rather Imitators than first Enterprizers of things where there is not a present

* Camden's History of Elizabeth.

† " Memorial of divers Merchants to Lords of the Council East India Trade," October, 1589.—Papers in India Office, quoted by Bruce.

‡ Sir William Monson, speaking of Raymond's voyage, says : " Their employment was to obstruct the Portuguese and to seize their goods by way of Letters of Reprisal," but the voyage was a failure, " for neither the men nor the Adventurers were a Penny the better for that voyage." A few of the survivors were brought home in a French pirate ship.

¶ Macpherson's Annals, Vol. II., pp. 200-201.

return of profit, etc."* The Portuguese had been already nearly a hundred years in India. They had made Goa the metropolitan city of all the East Indies. "The Vice Roy resides in this town, as does the metropolitan Bishop of the whole Indies."* The Spanish ships were already calling at the Indies on their homeward voyages from the new world. In an extract from a Spanish letter dated 1593 we see something of the hatred against the English and their attempts at trade, breaking out in the following strain. "They say at Seville that rather than they will permit Englishmen liberty of conscience in their country, or that they should trade to either of the Indies, they will sell their wives and children, and all else whatsoever, to withstand so unjust a demand.† Philip, in his efforts to crush the revolt in the Netherlands by shutting the Spanish ports to their vessels, only stimulated them to greater efforts. In 1595 a fleet of four vessels had sailed to Bantam and established the first warehouse of the Dutch in the East Indies. The success of this venture had resulted in the establishment of the "Society for Trade to distant Countries" (1597), which grew into the Dutch East India Company. The success of the Dutch, no doubt, was the immediate cause of the final organization of the London merchants, for they eyed jealously every progressive step of their neighbors and rivals.

* Monson's Naval Tracts.

† Extract from Correspondence, Spain, Sainsbury's Calendar State Papers, p. 97.

CHAPTER V.

THE COMPANY ORGANIZED.

"DIVERS merchaunts induced by the successe of the viage performed by the Duche Nation and beinge inforrmed that the duchemen prepare for a new viage, and to that ende have bought divers ships heere in Englande, were stirred with noe lesse affeccon to advaunce the trade of their native countrie, than Ye Duche merchaunts were to benefite theire commonwealthe, and upon yt affeccon have resolved to make a viage to the East Indias'"* is the way the acting Secretary of the Company recorded it, September 25th, 1599.† The memorial presented to Elizabeth is a lengthy, and for us not very interesting, document. Had our informant known the outcome of this step, he would have given us a little more of the details, and possibly have made use of a dictionary. The Company was to consist of a hundred shares, and stock aggregating £30,133 6s. 8d. was taken. But they were for some time unable to secure a charter from the Government. Elizabeth had not thought it prudent to defy the pleasure of the Spaniards by allowing her subjects to become their competitors in the East. Nothing could be done without royal consent, and with royal consent a company became a power. Mr. Froude, speaking of this period, says : ‡ " The officials

* The original document is yet in the India Office, Westminster, and was taken from the authorized records by the writer.

†" And this assemblie do electe, nominate and appoint thes fifteene persons hiervnder named comitties or directors of this viage to manage order and direct the affaires belonginge to the same as well concerning sewte to be made to her Majesty for sole privelegeto be granted to there adventurors for so manie yeres as can be obteyned and for such immunities and freedomes of Custome, &c."—Records in India Office.

‡ Froude's History of England, Vol. VIII., p. 424.

of the London companies ruled despotically in every English harbor; not a vessel cleared for a foreign port, not a smack went out for the herring season, without the official license; and the sale of every bale of goods or every hundred weight of fish was carried on under the eyes of the authorities, and at prices fixed by Act of Parliament." Before another year had passed, however, "having founde her Majestie gratiously inclyned,"* the Company was fully organized, and its stock-holders thirsting for the fortunes which they hoped their ships would bring from over sea; as it stands in the old document, "wherevppon the said adventurors in full and ample number assembled . . . did geave ther generall Consent by erecting of hands that they would *goe forward* in the said viage."

A very characteristic bit of information has been handed down to us† concerning the application for the employment of a member of the nobility. Some friends of one Sir Edward Michelborne petitioned the Company that he be employed in their first voyage. Their reply was, "in the behaulf of Sr Edward Michelborne to be employed in the viage as a principall Comaunder . . . noe further to vrge the imployment of this gent to the Companie, and to geave them leave to sort ther business with men of ther owne qualety, lest the suspeccon of the employment of *gentlemen* being takin hold upon by the generalitie, do dryve a greate number of the Adventurers to withdraw their contributions." Queen Elizabeth seems to have given her private consent before she felt at liberty to give public recognition by granting them the charter. It was not until the last day of December of the same year (1600) that the charter was granted to "The Governor and Company of Merchants of London trading to the East Indies." They were granted the usual privileges of corporations of that time, with powers to purchase and

* Records in India Office.
† Records, September 23rd, 1600.

dispose of land, etc. No others of the Queen's subjects were permitted to interfere with their trade under penalty of forfeiting ships and cargoes; half of their property thus confiscated going to the Company, the other half to the Queen. Their privileges were exclusive for a period of fifteen years, and gave them permission to export as much as £30,000 each voyage. The first four voyages their goods were to be exempt from all export duties.

The Company evidently foresaw some of the difficulties they would have to meet; before they had arranged for their voyage we find this minute of the proceedings (Feb. 10th, 1601). " It is ordaynened and decred that all preparation of moneis merchandizes and other provision for this present voyadge ... shal be holden reputed and accoupted and be carried maunaged, ordered and handled as one entyre Joynte and Comon Stocke of Advanture wherein no private traffique, barter, exchaunge or merchaundizinge shal be vsed, practized, or admytted by any factor, Mr. marrener officer or other person whatsoever employed in the saide voiadge, &c."*

Notwithstanding the anxiety to plunge into the Indian trade, when it actually came to the test of paying over their cash, India seemed to get farther away. The stockholders were slow about paying in their subscriptions; this was probably heightened by the Directors paying out large sums of money preparing for their first voyage. (March 6th,) " It appereth by the said estimat as the state of the Adventure as it standeth at this day that ther is owing by this Company aboute the Somme of IX m l." (£9,000). In April, the Company was in default to the extent of £7,000 and made an appeal to the Privy Council for special permission to deal with those that " Shewe themselves remisse and vnwillinge to furnyshe there promyssed contribucons," and the special powers asked for were granted them. They had some time before (Jan. 11th) had some such power granted, as we may conclude from the following paragraph: " Suche as shall

* Records in India Office.

refuse the same to Comitt them to prison vntil they conforme themselves and made satisfaction according to their subscriptions." Still the warrant seems not to have been drawn up until April 22nd. At length the more ambitious paid in the money according as they wished to invest and profiting or losing in the same ratio. Captain Lancaster with four ships and a pinnace set sail from Torbay, May 2nd, 1601.* The ship once on its way the ardor of those who had not invested cooled. Their money that had been subscribed to the capital stock came in still slower. The Queen's attention was called to the fact, and a letter was received from the Privy Council expressing their surprise at the Company's inactivity (Oct. 1601) and that her Majesty had supposed they would, as did the Dutch, equip fleets annually. But the Company evidently wanted to wait until they saw the results of their first venture. Nor was a second voyage undertaken until the ships returned from their first trip to the Orient. At length a man came riding into London at full gallop, the bearer of important news to the London merchants. One of the ships had just sailed into Plymouth and the generous Directors paid him £5 " for his paines ryding hither with the first report (June 16, 1603) of the coming of the *Assention* out of the Indies " as the Secretary recorded it. We can well imagine there was much rejoicing when at length the ships found their way up the Thames, and the curious crowd stood along the banks with wondering eyes, as they speculated on the riches that must make up their cargo. Then there was the letter to the Queen from the King of Java. Over many a pot of ale the exciting incidents of their voyage, the capture of the Portuguese ship, the dealings with the dark-skinned natives,

---

* The Records are very complete concerning the preparation of this first voyage. In making ready the ships we find a record " to allowe them of the Companies charge a barrell of beare everie day and to have a speciall care they leave not their worke to Runne to the Alehouse." Again as to equipments : "one dozen platters, two steepe tubbs, two firkins with tallowe, one fawkenett ladle, one great baskett for brad, six small basketts for head and sponge, &c."

their habits, customs, mode of living, etc., were recounted, over and over again. The most common sailor connected with the enterprise was a hero among his little circle of admirers. Nor was it any wonder that those who had invested heavily in the enterprise stroked their beards complacently trying to assume a careless air, yet with a bearing of "I told you so," for their profits were over 100 per cent. Nor did they concern themselves as to just how legitimately their proceeds were won. Sir William Monson,* writing a few years later, says: "And moreover in the forty-third year of the Queen and the year before she dy'd she granted a Patent to certain merchants for fifteen years Trade to the East Indies, which was prolongued in the ninth year of King James to continue forever; but the Queen liv'd not to see the return of that first voyage which Captain Lancaster went, and moreover, his employment was as well to Take by Violence, as to trade by Sufference, and unworthy the Name of an honest Design, for the Hands of Merchants should not be stained or polluted with Theft, for in such case all people would have liberty to do the like upon them." But we must remember that we are at present doing with the opening of the 17th Century, when English Protestants thought they were serving their religion whenever they were able to swoop down on a Catholic nation's ships, or seize upon the goods of the non-Christian nations.

* Naval Tracts.

These early records are very interesting. For example they began early to make provision against private trade (November 22nd, 1600). "It is ordered by the generall consent of this Assemblie that all factors imployed in this voyage shall geave securytie to the lykinge of the Comitties before he be putt in to ani charge, that he shall performe all faithful service to the generaltie and shall abstaine from all private trade."

One may gain from the following some idea of the presents sent out for native princes (January 17th, 1600): "It is ordered that two faire costlie Looking Glasses shal be provided to be geaven away as presents yf cause do require."

Another account shows their way of evading the question of piracy (January 22nd, 1600): "Whereas this assemblie were acquainted that ther hath bene some question made by some of the mariners what allowance they should have vppon such reprisalles as may happen in the voyage. It is vppon that question answered that there is noe intention to make anie attempts for reprisalles but onlie to pursue the voyage in a merchant-like course. Yet notwithstanding yf anie opportunity be offered wthout prejudice or hassard of the voyag Captain Lancaster is to take suche corse theren as he shall thinke meet and thervppon to make suche agrement wth the mariners for shares as he thinketh good. vppon such opportunity yf any suche happen."

January 11th, we find a note to the effect that no member be allowed to speak on a question " abowe three sundry tymes vppon peine of forfeiture of 3s. 4d. for every such excesse in speach."

Another extract which is taken from Sir William Monson's " Naval Tracts " shows their speculations as to the origin of gold and as to the color of the natives in the East : " The Sun rising to the Eastward betwixt the two Tropicks runs its course Westward over Asia and Africa till it come to the Ocean Sea, in which circuit its extream heat engenders the rich metal of Gold and changes the Complection of creatures to a Black hue, which the Heat reflects from the earth."—Vol. III., p. 392, Collection of Voyages and Travels.

CHAPTER VI.

UP TO THE MASSACRE OF AMBOYNA.

CAPTAIN LANCASTER had sailed to Sumatra, arranged with the natives a commercial treaty, then in route towards the Moluccas had taken a Portuguese ship. He then changed his course and came to Java, where he was so favorably received, that he established on this island the first agency of the Company. In the second voyage commanded by Captain Middleton, one ship was lost. Although he did not establish any new stations his cargo realized a handsome profit to its owners. The result of these adventures was a tempting bait to some of those who were not in the Company. Sir Edward Michelborne,* placing himself at the head of a few men of like opinion, succeeded in obtaining from King James (1604) the right to trade to Cathaia, China and Japan, Corea, Cambaia, etc. The granting of this petition was a direct violation of the charter of Elizabeth. The Company at once set up a tremendous howl. Michelborne, however, proceeded on his trip, which proved to be nothing more or less than a pirate's cruise. He at length returned to London with a profitable cargo. With this voyage began the difficulties of the Company with, as they denominated them, the interlopers.

The third voyage,† commanded by one Keeling, realized

* The same man who had been recommended by the court to the Company and had been refused by them. See p. 28.

† A part of the cargo of this voyage consisted of cloves which cost (Bruce) £2,948 15s. and which realized in England the sum of £36,287.

In Lancaster's Voyages, edited by Mr. Markham for the Hakluyt Society, it is maintained that " Hamlet " and "Richard the Second" were performed by sailors of Keeling's ship, the *Dragon*. And Sir George Birdwood in his Report says : " The Company's sailors were possibly equally well-known to Shakspere."

according to Bruce a profit of 234 per cent. There were according to the records twelve voyages made up to the year 1617. The aggregate capital of these voyages was about £464,284, or an average of some £38,690 for each voyage. This sum had been invested as follows : for shipping stores and provisions £263,746, for bullion £138,127, and for merchandise only £62,411. The profits were computed to average 138 per cent. With these facts we need not wonder at the references made to wealth by Jonson * and Shakespere.*

In the meantime many interesting events had taken place. At the beginning, the Portuguese seemed to have fought strenuously against the English, as well as all others who

* *Mammon.* "Come on, Sir. Now you set your foot on shore,
In Nova Orbe. Here's the rich Peru,
Great Solomon's Ophir ; he was sailing to 't
Three years, but we have reached it in ten months.
This is the day wherein to all my friends I will pronounce,
Be Rich.
This day you shall be spectalissime.
You shall no more deal with the hollow dye
Or the frail card . . .
. . . . No more
Shall thirst of Solin or the covetous hunger of velvet make
The Sons of Sword and Hazard fall before
The Golden Calf.
No more of this ; You shall start up young Viceroys.
Be Rich."
—"Alchemist," Act II., Sc. I. (year 1611).

Fal. " I will be cheaters to them both, and they shall
Be exchequers to me : they shall be my
East and West Indies, and I will trade to
Them both."—" Merry Wives of Windsor," Act I., Scene
III., lines 64-66.

There is another reference in " Twelfth Night " showing how early (about 1601 or 1602) India was in everybody's mouth.

Mar. " He does smile his face into more lines than is in the new
map with the augmentation of the Indies : you have not
seen such a thing as 'tis." Act III., Scene II., lines
73-75.

Sec. Gent. " Our King has all the Indies in his arms,
And more and richer, etc."—" King Henry VIII.," Act
I., Scene I., lines 45-46.

There are at least half-a-dozen more references in Shakspere to India, Indian or Indies. See Shakspere Lexicon by Dr. Alex. Schmidt.

invaded their right of way around the Cape. This had led to repeated efforts to find a north-west or north-east passage many years before the English braved the sea by the African coast.* We may form some idea of the strife against the English from a letter written from Seville at the time (1604):† " Eighteen Englishmen have made themselves strong with the help of the Indians in the isle of Claro, which is between China and the East Indies; they were besieged by 500 Portugals, who could not prevail against them, which has caused great uproar in all that country."

It was not many years, however, until the Portuguese seemed willing to share their trade, probably wishing to combine against the Dutch, who were fast becoming the power in the Indian Seas. Sir William Monson says: " This voluntary offer made by the Portuguese, who hitherto could not be brought upon no account to grant us Trade, we must conclude they are driven to it rather through necessity than Love or other Respects, for they find the Intrusion and good Success of the Hollanders to be such as in time may hazard the Ruine and Subversion in the Indies, without the help of the English, who are best able to help them."‡

The business had increased sufficiently by the year 1608 to lead the Company to construct at Deptford on the Thames a Dock-yard. Monson observes that this was the time "of the increase of great ships in England."¶ The same year the servants

---

* The first under Henry VIII. " His letters patent to John Cabot and his three sons 1496 were for the discovery of this very route." Sebastian Cabot, Hugh Willoughby, Chancellor Frobisher (1576-78), all were bent on accomplishing the same.

† From Correspondence, Spain,—Calendar State Papers, p. 141.

‡ Naval Tracts.

¶ Sir George Birdwood in his Report gives us some idea of the shipping of the time. What should we think of such a fleet now? " At the date of Queen Elizabeth's death there were not more than four merchant ships in the kingdom of 400 tons each, and the whole number of ships was barely 150." It is claimed that there was a ship of 1,100 tons sent against the Armada, but there is some question; for speaking of the sixth voyage Monson, I think it is, observes that the Trades Increase (1,100 tons) was lost, and argues that such large ships are impracticable and should not be built.

of the Company in the East recommended the opening of trade with some points on the continent. Heretofore the voyages had been directed to the islands. This suggestion was carried out Dec., 1612, by erecting an establishment upon the King's Phirmaund (document or license of permission) at Surat. The force brought to bear against the interlopers seems to have availed. In 1609 a new charter was granted the Company from King James, and with exclusive privileges forever, reserving only the condition, that in case it should prove prejudicial for the nation, it should be revoked upon a three years' notice. This favorable recognition of the Company encouraged equipments on a larger scale to be made.

The same year that a warehouse, or factory, as the historians have chosen to designate these stations, was established at Surat, the Directors of the Company decided that from that time, all trade should be conducted on the joint-stock plan. This practically threw the management of the concern into the hands of the Governor and Directors. £429,000 were subscribed, with which it was decided to make four separate voyages. As a financial stroke this change in the management of the Company does not seem to have been a very great success. We find, taking the profits of these four voyages separately, that they average but 87½ per cent.* Attempts were made to open trade with Japan (1610) and with Persia (1614-15), but nothing of importance came of either attempt. Difficulties with the Portuguese at Surat culminated in their defeat off Swally. The English following up their advantage, the Portuguese viceroy sailed away to Goa.

There seems to have been made, about this time, on the part of the Dutch Government, an attempt to join forces with the English, thus putting an end to the rivalry in India. The plan was to amalgamate the two Companies by a joint subscription aggregating £1,200,000, basing this union on the capture of the Moluccas by the Dutch from the Spaniards.

* Bruce Vol. I., p. 166.

But the plan did not meet with favor among the English, who argued that war was altogether a State business, and not in harmony with commercial enterprises such as they intended to carry forward. Moreover it was not sound " commercial principles for two nations to join in monopolizing a trade to the exclusion of others, and moreover impracticable."*

In 1614 Sir Thomas Roe was sent out by King James as ambassador at the expense of the East India Company to the Great Mogul. We have a great many letters from this man, who seems to have been wise and most judicious. A contemporary says of him, " he understands the dispositions of men so exactly, could suit their humours so fully, observe opportunities and reasons of actions so punctually, keep correspondence so warily, wade thro' difficulties so handsomely, wave the pinch of a business so dexterously, contrive interests so suitably, that he was advised with concerning the most* important affairs of the kingdoms he resided in abroad, and admitted of the Privy Council while he lived at home, where his speech against the debasing of the coin at the council table will last as long as there is reason of state in the world, his settlement of trade as long as this is an island, and his Eastern MS. as long as there are books to furnish libraries, or libraries to preserve books."† Be this praise little or much overdrawn, it is probable that few men would have accomplished, in the face of such difficulties, his work so well. He had carried with him as presents a coach, knives, dogs, etc.

He writes from Adsmere, Jan. 25th, 1615: "... and after many compliments I delivered his Majesty's Letter, with a copy of it in Persian, then I showed my commission and delivered your Presents, that is the Coach, the Virginals,

* See Sir George Birdwood's Report, p. 210.
† Lloyd's "State Worthies," pp. 1036-37. Quoted by Sainsbury.
Sir Thomas Smythe, for so many years Governor and the moving spirit of the Company, had proposed him " as a gentleman of pregnant understanding, well-spoken, learned, industrious, of a comely personage, and one of whom there are great hopes that he may work much good for the Company."—Court Minute Book, III., p. 219, Sainsbury's Calendar.

the knives, a scarf embroider and a rich sword of my own." Again speaking of the King : " He came down into a court, got into the Coach, and into every corner of it, causing it to be driven about." Although "it was ten o'clock at night," he sent for Roe to put on his scarf and sword after the English fashion. He must have been delighted ; for the writer goes on: "and he walked up and down flourishing it, and has not since been without it." Nations were judged in those days, by the Oriental rulers, by the value of the presents which their representatives brought. One of the Jesuits was asked by the King if the English King " were a Great King that sent Presents of so small value." In the same letter Roe adds : " I think four or five casks of that wine (Redwine) will be more welcome than the richest jewel in Cheapside." It seems Roe had presented him with some wine, and the royal ruler never stopped until he was drunk.

The letters of this ambassador are full of good suggestions to the Company. He saw the fickleness of Indian policy.* He advised against acquisition of territory and military expense. " By my consent you shall never engage yourselves but at sea, where you are like to gain as often as to lose. The Portuguese, notwithstanding their many rich residences, are beggared by keeping of soldiers : and yet their garrisons are but mean. They never made advantage of the Indias since they defended them ; observe this well. It has also been the error of the Dutch who seek plantations here by the sword. They turn a wonderful stock ; they prole in all places ; they possess some of the best : yet their dead pays consume all they gain. Let this be received as a rule, that if you will profit, seek it at sea, and in quiet trade, for, without controversies, it is an error to affect garrisons and laud wars in India." He urged the Company to make trade profitably,

* "The friendship we have here is fickle, the trade unsettled, one day a grant to us, the next to the Portugal, as they are false so they fear both, and would and will at last join with the strongest."—Letter from Roe, January 30th, 1616.

by a wise choice of servants, choice of salable commodities, and the taking of stringent measures against those in their employ who traded on their own account. An ambassador was not the best sort of a representative at an Eastern court. "An ambassador lives not in fit honor here," he says in another of his letters. "A meaner agent would, among these proud Moors, better effect your business. . . . Half my charge shall corrupt all this court to be your slaves. The best way to do your business in it is to find some Mogul that you may entertain for 1,000 ruppees a year, as your solicitors at court. He must be authorised by the King, and then he will serve you better than ten ambassadors."*

He was untiring in his service to the Company, but he had to struggle against great odds. The Dutch were already the power of the East. They had grown rich and powerful, through their trade in the spices, which were great novelties in Europe and much sought after. The English had from Java obtained their proportion of pepper, but were largely prohibited from the trade in cloves, nutmegs, and the finer spices. Notwithstanding these drawbacks, the Company was at this time flourishing, its returns most gratifying, their shipping extensive and fortunate.

We append here a list of the commodities which have, we believe, not been published in any history of the India Company.†

"THE COMODITIES OF THE ESTE INDIES."

"Sinemonde, peper case, pepper callycowe, longe pepper, cloves, maces, nutmegges, ginger mirabolanes in conserve, mirabolanes drye, grene ginger, nutmegges in conserve, synamon water, camfyer, burrassie, gallingale, cardamente, red sandes (red sanderswood), white sandes

---

* Roe's Correspondence.

† I am indebted to Sir George Birdwood's Report for this list, which was taken from the original records by Mr. Noel Sainsbury of the Public Record Office.

(sandalwood), tamornydes, myrre, balsamum, momya (wax from mummies) masticke, peper in pickell, muske and syvitt, amber greise, amber blacke, Benjamyn fyne, Benjamyn course, lingum alloes, blew Indea (indigo) lacrya to die wethall, hard wax, turbythe, radix China, alloies Sicotrinan, spignard, oyle of maces, rubarbe, goom appopanare, gum Selapin, gum Elemne, castorium, opium, tacamihaca, tutia, boill Indies nuttes (cocoa nuts), silke in clothe, silk rawe, cloth of erva, paynted clothes, callycow clothe, oeanaznenas, bengallas, lynen clothe of fyner sort than callycow clothe of goulde pussellanas (porcelain) certain dishes and plates so-called, targattes, ffaunes, a stone called bazar, diamonds, rubyes, saffiers, esmeralds, pearles greate, seide of pearle, turkeis, callimas armaticus, incense zedoarya cubebes, quiltes of silke."

CHAPTER VII.

Including Account of Massacre of Amboyna and Events up to Charter granted by Charles II.

England and Holland were friends outside India, and for many years they were friends and allies there. Competition in the Eastern trade growing stronger began to excite warm jealousy among the Companies' agents, which must sooner or later blaze out into full enmity. At the end of 1616 the records and correspondence which have come down to us show that the English Company was in the full tide of prosperity; their stations in India increasing, their servants coping most successfully against the Portuguese, whom they defeated in almost every naval engagement; their energy and valor commending them to the native princes, so much that they were granted flattering concessions. The Great Mogul being so pleased with the push of their representatives as to " much applaud our people's resolution," and to lead him to affirm that " his country was before us, to do therin whatsoever ourselves desired." Quite naturally the Dutch looked upon these rapid strides with disfavor, their jealousies kept brewing. The Dutch had established (1617) a station in Surat, the center of the English trade, and were rapidly extending their trade along the Coromandel coast. They had from the start held the monopoly of the spice islands. The letters of the English factors begin to be filled with complaints against their former friends and allies, rather than against their old enemies the Spaniards and Portuguese. The fact was, the Spaniards and Portuguese were becoming but passive rivals, while "the Flemmings thunder it loud in these parts," writes the President of one of the English stations (1618)."*

* March 18th of this year, Lord Bacon became a member of the East India Company.

Open hostilities soon commenced. The English took possession of Polaroon and Rosengin, more or less connected with a group of islands which were largely under the control of the Dutch. They at once laid claim, but the English had so well intrenched themselves that they could not easily be dislodged.

By way of retaliation, the Dutch seized two English ships and towed them into one of their settlements. They refused to release them until the English had evacuated the islands. The Dutch Company (1618) presented a memorial to King James, setting forth their grievances. This was immediately followed by a reply from the English Company, filled with their complaints against the Dutch. At length the two governments took the matter in hand, appointed representatives, who met in London and concluded a treaty (July 17th, 1619).* This treaty is a vague, indefinite document, showing conclusively that those who framed it had little just conception of how affairs must go in India. The two companies were to work in harmony, uniting their fleets for mutual protection, and their diplomacy for the exacting of greater privileges from the native princes. A "Council of Defense" was nominated, consisting of four members from each company to go out to India and see to the proper execution of this treaty, which was to remain in force for the period of twenty years. This practically meant the leaving of the conditions in India just as they had been, the stronger party taking every advantage, which meant that the Dutch would manage things about as they liked, since they were by far the stronger party. Although competing with all their strength and not always to their own advantage with their rivals, as we have seen, the English found time to extend in another direction their operations. In 1618-19

---

* The news of this treaty was gladly received in India "before any more Christian blood was spilt, and heathens to stand laughing at us and make benefit of our dissensions."—Letter from Sir John Rowe to Sir Thomas Smith, President India Company, May 2nd, 1620.

arrangements were made with Persia. It was advised that a few dogs, horses, etc., should be sent out to distribute as presents. The Portuguese were defeated in a naval engagement, and this was followed up by the combined force of the Persians and English attacking (April 22nd, 1622) and taking the island and city of Ormus, the center of the Portuguese trade to Persia. A part of the plunder (estimated at £100,000) taken from the Portuguese station, and half the customs at the port of Gombroon were made over to the English* in return for their services.

Some idea of the power the Company was already wielding may be seen from a statement taken from " Foedera " †:—
" The English East India Company, sending out six ships in the year 1618 for India, under the command-in-chief of Sir Thomas Dale,‡ King James, to add the greater weight to that voyage, granted him a special commission to govern that fleet, as well by common as by martial law; also to seize on the ships and merchandize of any others of his subjects who should be found navigating within the Company's

---

* Quoted from Rymer's "Foedera," Vol. XVII., p. 56, by Macpherson in his Annals.

† When the news of this great booty reached England, the King and the Duke of Buckingham, Lord High Admiral, each demanded shares in the Company, the one as droits of the Crown, the other as droits of the Admiralty, as well as a part of the prize money taken by the Company's ships, especially of that taken at Ormus. The Company squirmed. They did not wish to pay over the money; nor did they like calling down upon their heads the wrath of Royalty. It was referred to the Judge of the Admiralty Court, and according to Mill, the Duke received £10,000; whether a like sum was ever paid to the King we do not know. There has not yet been found any record in proof of it.

‡ Sir Thomas Dale made his name in different parts of the globe. He was at one time a military commander in the service of the States General of the United Provinces, was some time Governor of Virginia in America, and was now made Admiral of the largest fleet which up to this time had been sent out to India by the Company. He had returned from his port in America in 1616 " from the hardest task that he ever undertook," but says he left the colony " in great prosperity and peace, contrary to men's expectations." It was Dale who brought the celebrated Indian girl Pocahontas, along with some ten or twelve other natives, to England.

limits without their license, half the value of such seizures to belong to the crown and the other half to the Company."

But we must return to the rivalry between the English and the Dutch. The treaty was proving a failure, and animosities were fast approaching a crisis. This came in the form of a massacre at Amboyna (Feb., 1623). At this station, Captain Towerson, nine Englishmen, nine Japanese and one Portuguese sailor were accused of a conspiracy against the Dutch, tried and executed. We have many of the details of this massacre which show us the cruelty of the perpetrators. They resorted to what was even at that late date a practice too often brought into use, the horrors of the torture, to extract evidence in proof of their charges. From an old manuscript* in the British Museum the following particulars have come down to us: "The manner of his torture was as followeth:—First they hoisted him up by the hands with a cord upon a large door, where they made him fast upon two staples of iron fixed on both sides at the top of the door posts, hauling his hands the one from the other as wide as they could stretch. Being thus made fast his feet hung some two feet from the ground, which also they stretched asunder so far as they would reach, and so made them fast beneath into the door-trees on each side. Then they bound about his neck and face a cloth, so close that little or no water could go by. That done they poured the water softly upon his head, until the cloth was full up to his (the) mouth and nostrils and somewhat more (higher), so that he could not draw breath, but he must withal suck in the water; when he had drunk his body full, then began his pain for then the water (which) being still continued to be poured on (in) softly, forced all his inward parts, came out at (of) his nose (ears) and eyes, and often as it were stifling and choking him at length took away his breath and brought him to a 'swounde' and (or) fainting. Then they took him down

* I quote this from the Report of Mr. Sainsbury, of the Public Record Office, who took it from the MS.

quickly and made him vomit up the water. Being a little recovered, they triced him up again and poured in (the) water as before: eftsoons taking him down as he seemed to be stifled. In this manner they handled him three or four several times with water, till his body was swollen twice or thrice as big as before, his cheeks like great bladders, and his eyes staring and strutting out beyond his forehead. . . . (not confessing) wherefore they cut off his hair very short as supposing he had some witchcraft hidden therin. Afterwards they hoisted him as before, and then burnt him with lighted candles in the bottom of his feet until the fat dropped out the candles, yet then applied they fresh lights unto him. They burnt him also under the elbows, and in the palms of his hands, likewise under the arm pits, until his inwards might evidently be seen.

"At last, when they saw he could of himself make no handsome confession, then they lead him along with questions of Particular circumstances by themselves framed. . . . Having thus martyred this poor man they sent him out by four blacks, who carried him between them to a dungeon, where he lay five or six days without any 'chirurgeon' or other to dress him, until his flesh being putrefied great maggots dropt and crept from him in most noisome and loathsome fashion. Thus they finished their Sabbaths Day's work."

Can we wonder that the news of such an atrocity, although almost a year in reaching England, should at once arouse national indignation. London was wrought up to the highest pitch. The whole narrative was communicated to the King and Lords in Council, "whereat," says the Holland correspondence, "sundry of the greatest shed tears." The press teemed with articles painting the deed in blackest colors. The Company had a picture prepared depicting all the imaginable horrors connected with it.* The English

* Mill says, and upon good authority, that the English should not have made such a to-do, since they were themselves not strangers to the torture, and that the Company itself was "in the regular habit of perpetrating

claimed it was only a pretence on the part of the Dutch in the East to exterminate their factors from that part of India. The friends of the Company constantly maintained that there was absolutely no foundation for the accusations brought against Captain Towerson and his unfortunate associates. The Dutch, on the other hand, claimed that there did exist some sort of a conspiracy. I find nothing in the records so far as I have sought which proves that there was anything definite determined upon at Amboyna. Prof. Wilson says:—

"It is not impossible that there was amongst the English in Amboyna some wild scheme for the seizure of the island. The Japanese were soldiers of the garrison, and their position rendered their co-operation of an importance more than equivalent to the smallness of their numbers. At the same time, the conspirators were punished with a severity wholly unjustifiable. It is no extenuation of the cruelty of the Dutch to argue that the English in India in those days were guilty of similar atrocities, the fact is not proved, and the probability may be questioned: no instance of such savage barbarity can be quoted against any of the English factories or governments, and particular acts of severity towards deserters and pirates are not to be confounded with the deliberate cruelties of a public body . . . The conduct of the council of Amboyna admits of no doubt, and no plea of precedent or necessity can be justly heard in its palliation."*

The King gave orders detaining the Dutch fleet until satisfaction should be made by them. The Dutch Government for answer granted permission to the English to leave any and all their stations without paying any duties, and that all

tortures upon their own countrymen and even their own servants—of torturing to death by whips or famine." With their martial law, their right of capturing and punishing pirates, according to Hamilton ("New Account of East Indies"), they "whipt deserters out of this world into the next." These facts only show us the state of their way of dealing with criminals in those days.

* Prof. Wilson, of Oxford, quoted by D. Nolan in his "British Empire in India," Vol. II., p. 3.

disputes should be referred to the "Council of Defense," but that administrative powers whether civil or criminal should remain in their hands in all places acknowledging their jurisdiction, and to them belonged the exclusive right of Amboyna, the Bandas and the Moluccas. The claims of the English received little satisfaction. We shall find presently how often the English sought reparation and how they were put off by the Dutch.*

About this time (1624), the Company were granted the full right of martial as well as municipal law, regarding the handling of their servants in India. It is a curious thing that the English folk, so filled with the thought of individual freedom, should grant without any show of hesitancy such powers to a private corporation.

We have, we trust, given enough of the details during the first quarter of a century of the Company's existence to give the reader a fair knowledge of what the Company was as a trading concern. From this point we will pass more hastily over the remainder of that period during which the Company was simply a mercantile establishment. We shall only blaze the way by noting the chief events, giving enough, however, as we hope, to enable us to follow every progressive step made by the Company. The Second Joint Stock was issued in 1617, and its subscribers included 313 merchants and 214 tradesmen.†

Trade in Persia never proved very productive after the first few years. Stations in Siam and Japan were abandoned. When Charles I. came to the throne he seems to have been too much engrossed in other matters during the first year to heed any of the petitions of the India Company. The organization was not very prosperous; our records concerning

* We must bear in mind that the Dutch Company had many members who were government officials, while the English, for the most part, were merchants.

† The list mentions thirteen ladies of title, fifteen dukes and earls, twenty-five foreign merchants, eighteen widows and virgins, twenty-six doctors of divinity and medicine, eighty-two knights, etc.

a number of voyages are very imperfect. England was greatly burdened by the debts of James I. In 1631-32 a subscription for a third joint stock was opened and some £420,700 were subscribed. This revived to a certain extent the affairs of the Company. Trade with Persia was renewed. Surat, which was a presidency in 1612, became now the center of the English trade. The Company by accident more than sagacity discovered that their own affairs were constantly being overlooked by their employees, who busied themselves more with making fortunes for themselves than for the Company. The King granted them a proclamation which he issued " for restraining the excess of the private or clandestine trade, carried on to and from East Indies, by officers and sailors in the Company's own ships."* In 1632-33 there arose in England a great cry against monopolies, Sir William Courten taking advantage of this public opinion, and the fact that the English and Portuguese had determined to be friends in India, admitting each other freely to their factories, organized a new company. The King accepted stock† and granted a license to the organization (Dec. 12th, 1635). His excuse for violating the charter of King James was the mismanagement and the neglect on the part of the old company to fulfil the conditions of their charter.

Ships were sent out and returned, yielding large profits. The old company unceasingly petitioned, complained, pled, threatened, until finally the King promised to withdraw the license, but it was never carried into effect. Charles was becoming more and more involved with his Parliament. He had no money to prepare for the contest that was coming on. It occurred to him to make something out of the India Company. He sent and bought up all the pepper in the Company's magazines on credit, sold it for a reduced price for cash, yielding him something over £50,600. The bonds

* Bruce.
† Mill, Vol. I., p. 42.

he gave the Company were never fully paid off. In 1633-34 a Phirmaund had been obtained granting privileges of trade in Bengal. A few years later (1639)* a fortified factory at Madras was begun. During the civil war in England little effort was made in the direction of their trade, fearing one party or the other would seize upon their goods. The Dutch had followed up the example of the English by coming to mutual terms (1644) with the Portuguese. The next year they sailed with a large fleet into the Persian Gulf, and succeeded in winning favourable terms from the Persians. Courten's Association, which had thriven largely through its seizures rather than legitimate trade, yielded less satisfactory returns.

The Council of State recommended the union of the Assada merchants, as Courten's Association was called, with the old company, which was accordingly done (Nov., 1649).† When Cromwell came into power, he very soon reduced the Dutch to such extremity that they were willing to accede to his own terms.‡

A Commission was appointed which met in 1654, to at length adjust the difficulties which had stood between the English and the Dutch Companies for over forty years. The English laid claims to damages aggregating £2,695,999 15s.¶, but this was no difficulty to the Dutch, who at once presented a counter-claim amounting to £2,919,861 3s. 6d. The whole matter was settled by allotting to the English £85,000 and

* Wheeler.

† Bruce.

‡ " At this period (1645-50), however, the trade of the Company suffered great depression, owing to the ascendency of the Puritan party in England, affecting the home demand for silks, figured stuffs and other denominations of artistic price goods ; and to rumours of the civil war in England having at length reached the East, the Company was seriously injured thereby, particularly in Persia, where ' the tragicall storye of the Kinge's beheadinge made a deep and lasting impression'."—Sir George Birdwood's Report, p. 217.

¶ Bruce.

£3,615 was awarded as reparation for the massacre of Amboyna. £50,000 was loaned to the Protector as a mark of "gratitude" by the Company. The Dutch, however, were fast outstripping the English in their operations in the East. The united joint stock does not seem to have been a great success; at any rate our records are very scant. After the Restoration, Charles II., who was more given to leading a gay life than to attending to serious questions of state, readily granted a new charter (April 3rd, 1661): "That they should, forever hereafter, have, use, and enjoy, the whole, entire and only trade and traffic to and from the East Indies." It was exclusive like those of Elizabeth and King James, and was, like that of the latter, to continue indefinitely.*

*Bruce.

CHAPTER VIII.

UP TO THE UNION OF THE TWO COMPANIES.

THE charter granted by Charles II. contained two important privileges: the authority to make peace and war with non-Christian people; and to seize all unlicensed persons found within the Company's limits. The Company was thus early in its history vested with almost full powers of government.

This period is one of considerable interest. Our records are fairly complete, and contemporary writers begin to make frequent references to the Company's affairs. Milton, in " Paradise Lost ",* refers to India. Pepys† tells about being carried down into the hold of an Indian ship, "and there did show me the greatest wealth lie in confusion that a man can see in this world."

According to Bruce the first order for tea was made by the Company in 1668: "To send home by these ships 100 lbs. waight of the best tey that you can gett." Some had reached England earlier, however, for Pepys in his diary writes (September 25th, 1660): "I did send for a cup of tee (a chinea drink) of which I had never drunk before." This is the first reference made to the plant by any English writer

---

* Milton says, describing Satan's flight:
  " Hangs in the clouds, by equinoctial winds
  Close sailing from Bengala, or the isles
  Of Ternote and Tidore, whence merchants bring
  Their spicy drugs."—" Paradise Lost," Book II., 637-40.
Again he must have had India in mind when he says:
  " As when to them who sail
  Beyond the Cape of Hope, and now are past
  Mozambic, off at sea north-east winds blow
  Sabean odors from the spicy shore
  Of Araby the Blest."—Book IV., 159-63.

† Diary, November 16th, 1665.

so far as we know. According to Sir George Birdwood's Report, the Company purchased and presented to Charles II. two lbs. of tea in 1664, and four years later 23 ¾ lbs.; and the first consignment was made from India from Bantam in 1669; 143¼ lbs. were received. In 1666 the Great London Fire destroyed all the saltpetre warehouses, and all the pepper stored away in the vaults under the Royal Exchange met the same fate. Although there was probably more talk about the East India Company than all other companies combined, it was not the most important as to actual returns. Mill says:—* "the English fishery at the single station of Newfoundland exceeded the value in every respect of the trade to the East Indies." Anderson in his Introduction† says:—" That although our own present East India Company enjoys an extensive trade, and is, seemingly, having many fine forts and factories, and a considerable territorial property, in India, making also at home considerable dividends, and such immense sales, too, as were never known in former times, having also of late years adorned even the city of London itself, not only with a fine office,‡ but with such spacious and numerous warehouses, as perhaps are scarcely equalled in any other nation : all which are likewise their own property. Yet with respect to all Europe complexly taken, it seems to be universally agreed to be a pernicious trade: a trade draining it of all or most of the silver which America brings to it. . . . If all Europe, therefore, could be supposed jointly to agree in dropping the East India trade entirely, it

* Mill, British India, Vol. I., p. 67.

† Anderson's History of Commerce.

‡ Locations of Company's Office: From 1604-21 the headquarters of all the Company's business were at the house of the first Governor, Sir Thomas Smythe, in Philpot Lane ; 1621-38 in Crosby Hall, Bishopsgate Street, belonging to Lord Northampton ; 1638 in the house of Governor Sir Christopher Clitheroe in Leadenhall Street ; 1648 removed to adjoining house. In 1726 a new front was added ; entirely reconstructed in 1796. In 1858, passing to the Crown, was removed to Westminster Palace Hotel ; 1860-67 to its present quarters by St. James' Park.—Birdwood's Report.

would be better for the whole, as well as every particular nation in it." And then, strange as it may seem, he adds: "We must ever be of opinion that our East India trade, under its present circumstances, is really a beneficial one for Great Britain." Such was the expressed sentiment, not only of this celebrated writer, but, as well, of a large body of the English folk at this time. There were probably many causes leading up to this opinion. There was threatened trouble with the Mahrattas in India; difficulties with the Dutch:* " By the way 'tis observable ye Dutch omit no opportunity to do us all the prejudice that lyes in their power ".† The Company had not kept up its reputation in the East. On one occasion when they had asked some concession of duties, the native prince replied: "When the English horns and teeth grew he would then free them from the duty." Hedges says:‡ " The nabob commanded him to begone out of his sight, saying, ye English were a company of base quareling people, and foul dealers."

Even at this late date piracy seems to have flourished among the English, although Wheeler says, referring to efforts to suppress it: " No Englishman, however, could be condemned to death unless convicted of piracy, which was

---

* (1674, March 13-26th, Cor. II.) "That whereas in persuance of articles of agreement, and under the Great Seal of 27th October, 1673, between Prince Rupert, Duke of Cumberland, and others, His Majesty's commissioners of Prizes, and the East India Company, touching East Indian goods lately taken from the Dutch in the four ships,—which were put in the Company's hands to be disposed of to His Majesty's most advantage. Said company has disposed of said goods for the sum of £174,740 9s. 8d. and have paid the same to His Majesty's use. His Majesty by these presents doth remise, release, and forever quit claim unto said East India Company and successors all suits, claims and demands against said Company concerning said sum of money and goods."—In Public Record Office, quoted by Mr. Sainsbury.
Again: " Reciting articles of agreement of 7th of November, 1665, and touching goods taken from two Dutch East India ships—sold and disposed of for His Majesty's use for the sum of £154,969 13s. 6d."—Ibid.

† Sir William Hedges' Diary, October 10th, 1682.

‡ The same, July 25th, 1684.

regarded as the most heinous of crimes."* If we may accept as evidence a contemporary letter written from London, we must conclude that piracy was not such a " heinous crime : " " How brave they are at sea plainly appears by that great Spanish Armada called the Invincible, which they, with a small number of ships, ruined in the reign of Queen Elizabeth. . . . They trade in all parts of the world, but in such manner that it may well be said of their ships that they are one half furnished for war and the other half for trade, for there are none of them but what will play the pyrates at the Canaries, Brazil, Cabo Verde and the West Indies, and they are so fond of this infamous gain, that many sell all they have to purchase a ship and set out robbing."†

In the Orient a new rival appeared, destined to seriously endanger the interest of the English. This new rival was a French company. The French had long aspired to make themselves strong at sea, and had, so early as 1609, set on foot a plan to trade to the East Indies.‡ The plan was only carried into execution in 1665-66, by the great financier of Louis XIV, Colbert, who was president of the organization. A fleet was sent out and a station founded at

* In the old Madras records the reference made to the punishing of pirates illustrates what was characteristic of the time : " The Court Martial upon the 12th instant, having tried the nine Englishmen sent us by the Dutch Commissary from Pulicat, and finding them all guilty of piracy, though not all equally culpable : therefore it was concluded by majority of votes to condemn two to death, and six to be branded in the forehead with a " P," which six was to have been branded to-day but the marshall being sick it is ordered to defer the execution till to-morrow ; and that two of them be branded at the execution post under the fort point and that the guards be drawn up to be spectators of the sad example. The other four to make their punishment more exemplary and to terrify others . . . it is ordered that two be branded aboard the " Williamson " and the other two aboard the " Revolution."—Wheeler's " Madras in the Olden Time " (April 15th, 1689).

† Dr. John Francis Gemelli Cureri, writing to the Councillor, Amato Danio.

‡ Extract from Correspondence, France, 1609.

Pondicherry.* We shall see how in less than half a century they plan the conquest of India.

In 1684 the English were expelled by the Dutch from Java; in 1688 the first post-office was established.† During this period Sir Josiah Child was the Governor ‡ of the East India Company at home, and was its prime mover. Burnet (Bishop of Salisbury), says of him :¶ "He was a man of great notions as to merchandise, which was his education, and in which he succeeded beyond any man of his time; he applied himself chiefly to the East India trade, which by his management was raised so high that it drew much envy and jealousy both upon himself and upon the Company; he had a compass of knowledge and apprehension beyond any merchant I ever knew; he was vain and covetous, and thought too cunning, though to me he seemed always sincere." He doubtless inspired the following sentiments of the Directors in 1689, for he was something of a statesman : " The increase of our revenue is the subject of our care, as much as our trade,"—our first record of the Company's looking to political power save only for purposes of trade. And this, which seems quite prophetic, is attributed to the same far-seeing man: "That which we promise ourselves in a most especial manner from our new President and council, is that they will establish such a Politie of Civill and military power, and

---

* First French company planned in 1604.
  Second   ,,   ,,   ,,   1611.
  Third   ,,   ,,   ,,   1615.
  Fourth, under Richelieu   ,,   1642.
  Fifth, under Colbert   ,,   1664.
  Sixth, Union of E. and W. India Co., and other Company, 1719.

† Elihu Yale, the benefactor of Yale College in America, was nominated a writer, 11th of November, 1670·; arrived at Fort St. George, 1672; was made a factor in 1679; promoted to member of the Council in 1685; appointed Governor, July 25th, 1687, and held the post five years. His son, David, died in India January 26th, 1688. He left India 1699.

‡ 1685-86, Sir John Child, brother of the President of the Company, was made "Captain General and Admiral" of all the Company's forces. He ably seconded his brother in London.

¶ "History of His Own Time."

create and secure such a large Revenue to maintain both at that place, as may bee the foundation of a large, well grounded, sure English Dominion in India for all time to come."* Josiah Child ruled like an autocrat. The power of his wealth for a time knew no bounds. He had dropped into the purse of Charles a gift of ten thousand guineas. James was presented with three thousand more. Courtiers and their mistresses, churchmen, all who had influence at court,† " were kept in good humour by presents of shawls and silks, birds' nests and altars of roses, bulses of diamonds, and bags of guineas." The Company thrived under court patronage. But this was not to last. Trouble arose in India. James was driven from the throne. Parliament assumed greater powers. Provincial merchants had long cried out against these London monopolies. In 1691 opposition against the London Company took an organised form. London was kept in constant agitation. Petitions were poured in upon Parliament. The new company was popular, for there was strong feeling against the old. Popular opinion had changed. The new company's weapons were libels; the old wielded the stronger power of bribes. Child fought desperately. Parliaments usually move slowly. In the meantime, the pamphlet war and coffee-house strife did not abate. Two years later it seemed fiercer than ever. The old company became alarmed. This year (1693) the Company spent £90,000 in bribing the Privy Council to renew their charter, and to prevent the incorporation of the new company.‡ Nor was this the extent of their corrupting: " It was found that in the books of the East India Company there were entries of great sums given for secret service done the Company that amounted to £170,000, and it was generally believed that the greater part of it had gone among the members of the House

* Company's letter to Fort. St. George, December 12th, 1687. Diary of Sir William Hedges.
† Macaulay's Hist. of England.
‡ Birdwood's Report.

of Commons, ... yet this whole discovery was let fall, and it was believed, too many of all sides were concerned in it, for, by a common consent, it was never revived."* The charter, with some modifications, was sealed.

The Company was injudicious. Their acts against interlopers called forth a fresh outburst of wrath. Parliament "moved that all subjects of England had equal right to the East Indies unless prohibited by Act of Parliament," and the motion passed. Child's commands in India, however, were higher authority than Parliamentary acts, and beyond the Cape, merchantmen found it so unsafe as to make them not venture much of their wealth.

In 1695, in spite of all the vast sums spent in bribing, the Company lost by ten votes in Parliament, "so many of their friends being absent, going to see a tiger baited by dogs." 1698 came round. The old Company's exclusive privileges were no more. The contending faction again besieged Parliament. The old Company offered to loan the Government £700,000, if granted their old monopoly. The opposition was this time not to be put down. They offered to loan two millions at eight per cent. And the "General Society" trading to the Indies received its charter. The old Company had bought up £315,000 of the new stock. Notwithstanding, they tried to kill their rival. The new company was scarcely able to cope with the wealth and experience of the old. After fighting each other in every possible way, a union was effected and published 1708.

---

* Burnet's "History of His Own Times," Vol. IV, pp. 254-57.

Burnet gives us a glimpse of the celebrated pirate who was supposed to have buried on Long Island near New York City immense treasure. Referring to the report that some pirates were doing mischief in Indian seas, he says: "So a man of war was to be sent out to destroy them, and one Kid was pitched upon, who knew their haunts, and was thought a proper man for the service. . . The King preferred the managing it by private undertaking, and said he would lay down £3,000 himself." Since the money had been otherwise proportioned by Parliament, it was taken up by ministers, etc., but the King never paid his subscription. "When this Kid was thus set out, he turned pirate himself."—Vol. IV., pp. 422-23.

We have a most interesting sift of old India records, carefully collected and published by J. Talboys Wheeler, in a book which he calls " Madras in the Olden Time."* It is replete with the details of the early life in India. We are indebted to him, too, for facts which throw new life on a number of points of the earlier history of the Company. The factory, as a station is designated in the records, was simply a large warehouse, the lower floor being occupied for storage and for the office ; the upper floor forming the dining-room and sleeping apartments. The place was often a sort of fort. As the station grew in importance, the higher officials erected houses for themselves. Their rules were very strict, but as is almost invariably the case when humanity is bound down by stringent laws, various acts of disobedience constantly cropped out. A chaplain was usually sent out with a fleet of any importance, prayers were held morning and evening. No one was allowed to " be Drunke, to Swear, Lye, Quarrell, etc." In the factories prayers were said every morning, and there was a fine of 2s. 6d. for any who were absent week days, and five shillings on Sunday. For being drunk or abusing natives, one was " to be sett at the gate in Irons all daytime and all night to be tyed to a Post in the house." Staying out of the factory over night without permission was punishable by a fine of 4s. For many years no women were allowed to go out, as they could not from their mode of living very well provide for them. They whiled away their leisure hours as well as they could by various games. In a letter of the time we find one of the more industrious uttering his complaints about their attending cock-fighting and other games, "wherin they consume the half of their time to their great impoverishment."

* Thomas Pitt, grandfather of the Earl of Chatham, was Governor of Madras from 1698-1709. He bought, during his administration, the celebrated diamond which was sold to the Duke of Orleans for £135,000 sterling. This diamond has had an interesting history. It was the subject of some scandal at the time of Pitt, as we may gather from the following lines from Pope :

" Asleep and naked as an Indian lay
An honest factor stole his gem away."

CHAPTER IX.

INCLUDING AN ACCOUNT OF THE GERMAN COMPANIES.

WITH the union of the two companies, their combined wealth and influence made them a great power. A new era opens in the Indian trade. Their operations begin on a larger scale and are more regular. In India their forts grow into towns. The control of their stations is divided into three Presidencies, Madras*, Calcutta, and Bombay†. The power of each is independent as regards the other; responsible only to the Directors and Governor of the Company in London. This power is vested in each case in a President, and Council, consisting of from nine to twelve members. All acts must have been legalized by a majority of votes in Council; the influence however of the President was usually sufficient to carry with it the majority of the Council. In 1726 a charter was granted the Company which gave them the right to establish a mayor's court in each of the Presidencies. This court, to consist of a mayor and nine aldermen, was empowered to decide all civil cases. The President and Council were erected into a Court of Appeal with the power of exercising penal judicature excepting in case of high treason. There were also courts erected for the judging of questions arising among or with the natives within their jurisdiction; the Company thus taking it upon itself to act as judge in all cases which arose between it and other parties. The President was Commander-in-chief of whatever military forces there were. It was a motley lot that

---

* Secured from the native rulers.
† Ceded as a part of the dowry of Catherine of Portugal, and made over to the Company for an annual rental of £10 a year.

made up the English recruits. Deserters enlisted from every other nationality represented in India; half-breeds, and natives called Sepoys. "During the twenty years ending 1728 the average annual exports of the East India Company from England were £442,350 of bullion, £92,288 of goods. Average imports were valued at £758,042; chiefly calicoes and other woven goods, raw silk, diamonds, tea, porcelain, pepper, drugs, saltpetre, etc." * It was during this period that a new rival again appeared in the field to the great discomfiture of the Company. During the European period, if I may so designate it, of financial speculation, Austria, whose Emperor, Charles VI., was influenced largely by Prince Eugene, sought to build up mercantile adventures, and to extend her sea power at Trieste on the south and at Ostend on the north. As early as 1717, two ships had sailed away for the Indies from Ostend bearing passports from the Prince Eugene. Holland and England hastened to expostulate with the Emperor himself, and the question formed one of the most strongly contested points in the diplomatic relations of the time. But the Emperor had high hopes of great wealth filling his coffers from the Orient. The Dutch captured some of the Ostend ships, but they were not discouraged. The English claimed the rights of trade for the powers already in India. They were the prime movers in this work, and besieged Parliament, until an act was procured (1721) enforcing penalties already enacted, but its effect was not sufficient. Two years later another act was granted prohibiting foreign adventures to India, making the offence punishable to the extent of £1,500 for each offence. All British subjects found in India, not serving the English Company, or not holding license from the same, should be seized and sent home for punishment.

The Emperor, Charles VI., had not yielded to the repeated requests of the Ostend Company by granting them

* Sir William Hunter's "Gazetteer of India," p. 561.

a charter, fearing it would, in some way, make against his diplomatic hopes. They had traded as private individuals under Royal passports. December 17th, 1722, the charter at length received Royal recognition by its deed of institution. The stock, one million sterling, was at once taken, and within thirty days the same stock was at a premium of 15 %. But the one thing which was nearest the Emperor's heart was the recognition of all the powers to the Pragmatic Sanction, the securing of the succession of his daughter to his throne. At length he yielded, throwing over the Company in order to get England to recognize the succession. He agreed to suspend the business of the Company for seven years, and it was quite understood that it should cease to exist. There is in the India Office a volume of documents labelled "Ostend Company," but there is not a great deal in it of real historical worth. I find in a letter from Antwerp to Alexander Hume the following : " We have Received a Decree from her Serene Highness of the 11th of this month (1732) abolishing the Company, working the Octroy and putting a perpetual stop to the East India trade from the low Countrys : and as to the Factories his Majesty will let us know his intentions in time and Place."

In the Madras records we find something of how the opposition against the Germans was pushed in India : " The President acquaints the Board that he is advised the Ostend ship that was at Merga went lately to Pondicherry, but was denied the liberty of that Port : whence she went to Tranquebar, and obtained protection from the Danes, where she continues in order to procure a cargo for Europe, wherefore he proposes that the prohibition, hereafter entered, be published in all languages, to prevent all commerce or correspondence directly or indirectly with the Ostenders, or any concerned with them, which is unanimously agreed to." * The proclamation follows, a part of which I quote : " This is therefore to

* April 6th, 1731.—Wheeler.

give public notice that whatever inhabitant of this place shall aid or assist the said ship, in any manner of way, directly or indirectly, either by himself or by his servants or correspondence,—his estate shall be confiscated to the use of the Honorable Company and himself expelled the Bounds." This shows not only the fight which was made against those wishing to enter the Indian trade, but also shows us something of the power which was in the hands of the servants of the Company.

The Ostend Company, however, died hard. It became bankrupt in 1784 and was wholly done away with in 1793. About the time the Emperor gave up the Company, Frederick of Sweden (June 14th, 1731) granted to Henry König & Co. a charter for trade to the East. Its stock did not go very rapidly. A representation was sent to enlist the members of the Ostend Company. In a letter, a copy of which is in the India Office, the writer states the chief difficulty is " to have leave from the Emperor to Concern themselves in that trade which is forbidden them by one of the Articles in the Charter of the Ostend Company." It seems, too, there was some talk of removing the Ostend Company to Trieste. This was indeed the plan and advice of Prince Eugene, who had from the start urged the Emperor to concentrate his energies in making that city his chief point of trade, etc. " I am fully persuaded [in the same letter] that the court of Vienna has, at present, in view the translating the Indian Trade from Ostend to Trieste, and as I observed before, these People will never consent, that their stock should be Employed in that manner. This makes the Directors very uneasy and if they dared, they would give up their Employs."

In 1744, Frederick the Great, upon acquiring East Friesland, made an attempt to open up trade to the East. He gave his sanction to the Asiatic Trading Company (September 1st, 1750), which had a capital of £170,625. Some half-dozen ships sent out to China yielded 10 per cent. dividends, as a result of seven years' experience. It was Frederick's desire that Embden become a port of some importance.

In 1753, the "Bengalische Handelsgesellschaft" was founded. This company made two expeditions which did not yield happy results. It became involved in a lawsuit and had to suspend business. They had to contend with the combined force and influence of the French, Dutch and English. These spared no pains or labor to defeat any attempts made by the Germans to get a footing in India. They refused guides or pilots to them or "any other traders not belonging to powers already established in India," to show them through the dangerous places. Nor were these their only enemies; the natives opposed them. The native governor of Bengal wrote to the English:—" If the Germans come here, it will be very bad for all the Europeans, but for you most of all, and you will afterwards repent it, and I shall be obliged to stop all your trade and business.... Therefore, take care that these German ships do not come." And the English answered solemnly : " God forbid that they should come, but should this be the case, am in hopes they will be either sunk, broke, or destroyed." Notwithstanding all vigorous opposition, they found their way into Bengal, and found plenty of the factors of the Dutch and English Companies ready to exchange with them on their own private account in face of the orders of their superiors. The court had written: "If any of the Prussian ships want the usual assistance of water, provisions or real necessities, they are to be supplied according to the customs of nations in amity one with the other. But you are on no pretence whatsoever to have any dealings with them, or give the least assistance in their mercantile affairs."*

Sir W. Hunter thus ably sums up the results of powers to acquire something in India : " The Portuguese failed because they attempted a task altogether beyond their strength—the conquest and the conversion of India. Their

* Letter to Calcutta Council, March 25th, 1756, quoted by Sir William Hunter.

memorials are the epic of the Lusiad, the death-roll of the Inquisition, an indigent half-caste population and three decayed patches of territory on the Bombay coast. The Dutch failed on the Indian Continent because their trade was based on a monopoly which it was impossible to maintain, except by great and costly armaments. Their monopoly, however, still flourishes in their isolated island dominion of Java. The French failed in spite of the brilliancy of their arms, and the genius of their generals, from want of steady support at home. Their ablest Indian servants fell victims to a corrupt court and a careless people. Their surviving settlements declare that talent for careful administration, which, but for French monarchs and their ministers, and their mistresses, might have been displayed throughout a wide Indian Empire. The German companies whether Austrian or Prussian, were sacrificed to the diplomatic necessities of their royal patrons in Europe, and to the dependence of the German states in the wars of the last century upon the Maritime Power. But the German people has never abandoned the struggle. The share in the Indian trade which Prussian King and Austrian Kaiser failed to grasp in the 18th century, has been gradually acquired by German merchants in our own day.

An important part of the commerce of Calcutta and Bombay is now conducted by German firms. German mercantile agents are to be found in the rice districts, the jute districts, the cotton districts, and persons of German nationality have rapidly increased in the Census returns."

CHAPTER X.

Up to the Battle of Plassy.

WE have seen in a former chapter that the moving spirit of the East India Company had declared that, from that time on, they should make revenue a part of their care as well as extension of trade. Sir Josiah Child had advanced ideas. He it was, without doubt, who had drafted for Madras the plan of corporation which was instituted under the governorship of Yale, in 1688. From his palatial residence on the banks of the Thames, he planned a scheme of making war against the Mogul himself, and of making the English "a nation in India." But the times were not yet ripe for such an undertaking. The Company at the beginning of the 18th century seems to have settled down to its regular affairs. As we have seen, the union of the old and the new companies had been effected. Aurungzebe had died (1707) about the same time. He had been for half a century the great Emperor of India. He was the great-grandson of Akbar. From an early age he had devoted himself to religion, affecting to despise all earthly vanity. He combined all the cunning, deceit, treachery,* and shrewdness of his race. He spared neither treachery nor murder in raising himself to the throne, pretending all the while his ambition was to retire from public life and devote

---
* He was a descendant of Tamerlane. His father, Shah Jehan, had made himself secure on the throne by putting to death every male descendant of Tamerlane except members of his own family.

E

himself to their religious forms. Once on the throne he displayed many virtues. He was assiduous and impartial in dispensing justice. He showed considerable concern for the welfare of his people. In private life he stood far above the plain of Indian rulers. His great fault was his ambition, which stopped at nothing. In his later years he showed, as we gather from a number of letters, keen remorse for the crimes of his earlier life. With his death began the decline of the Mogul Empire. During the first half of the 18th century the English had little to do with the natives except in so far as their trade led them. The Indians were busy fighting among themselves. In the meantime Bombay had grown into quite an important point with shipping docks, with a post-office, insurance company, churches, and many of the accompaniments of the English civilization. Madras was probably a city of more importance on the Coromandel coast. Calcutta made the third important station in India. There had been, however, little change in the territorial relations of the Company. But the declaration of war between France and England was followed by important measures in India as well as in America.

Colbert's Company had had a long struggle to get a footing in India. At length a settlement was effected at Pondicherry, which grew into a prosperous trading center. On the Continent of India itself this was their only point of any considerable importance. The islands of Mauritius and Bourbon were under the control of the French and in a flourishing condition. M. Labourdonnais, the governor of these islands, was in France just before the declaration of war, and had been granted permission by the Government, though not by the Company, to make an attack on the British possessions in India. He was a man of large experience and practical ideas. He took his motley crew, adding to his force from every source possible, trained them to the use of the musket, and at the first intelligence of the declaration of war, he sailed to Madras, and after a five days' bombardment, the city capitulated (1746). Labourdonnais then returned to Pondicherry.

The governor of Pondicherry since 1742 was M. Dupleix, and to this French aspirant are to be traced some of the most important revolutions in India. He had been especially trained for commercial life; had gone out to India very early, and soon won the favorable opinion of the Company. His private fortune had enabled him to accumulate vast wealth by conducting an expensive private trade. He was of intensest energy, ingenious and ambitious, but he was vain and of a jealous disposition. He looked with disfavor upon the work which M. Labourdonnais was doing, especially did he protest against a condition of the surrender of Madras—that it should at the expiration of a certain time be restored to the English. The result was that M. Labourdonnais was unable to proceed farther with his plans, and soon after hastened to France to clear himself of charges hatched up against him by his enemies.*

Dupleix, left to himself, began the carrying forward of the plan of campaign begun by his rival. He was encouraged by defeating a large army of the natives with a handful of his own forces. His ambition rose as his imagination pictured out a French Empire in India with himself at its head. He plundered Madras and planned the taking of Fort. St. David, which, if it had been successful, would have left him almost without a rival in India. The Nabob of Arcot had come to aid the English. They surprised the French forces and obliged them to retreat. Dupleix next busied himself in winning over the Nabob, for Indian princes are ever ready to break an oath and join arms with the strongest side. This having been carried out by his receiving the son of the Nabob in Oriental pomp, Dupleix resumed his enterprise. An English fleet appearing with re-inforcements, the French retreated. The English now feeling themselves strong

---

* Upon his arrival he was unjustly thrown into the Bastille and did not long survive a three years' imprisonment.

enough to proceed on the offensive besieged Pondicherry. The work was not skilfully carried forward, and the rainy season coming on, the English had to withdraw from the siege, while the French gloried in what they considered a great victory. It was in this siege that young Clive distinguished himself by his bravery and daring. Then followed news of the treaty of Aix-la-Chapelle, and the full restoration of Madras to the English. And in India the French and English stood in the same relations as they did before the war, except in one respect ; each had an army, each had seen a large force of natives go down before a much smaller force of Europeans, each had seen that the natives might be taken and trained in the use of arms, according to the European methods. With India in its constant turmoil of change and decay, deposing and raising princes to the thrones by those who wielded military power, thus exposing to the foreigners their weakness and instability, it would be exactly what we should expect, if these outside powers each had armies which were idle, that they should very soon take part in some of the native conflicts. And so it came about, the English leading off, and assuming to act as a power in India. A prince of Tanjore who had been dethroned begged the English to reinstate him, offering them the district of Devi-Cotah and expenses of the war if they were successful. The place, upon the second attempt, was taken (1749), and here again Clive drew upon himself the admiration of his countrymen. The King in power conceded to the English Devi-Cotah with territory valued at 9,000 pagodas annually. Upon these terms the English renounced the support of the prince for whom they had taken up arms and agreed to keep him in security if allowed about £400 a year as pension for his expenses.

 The French had followed the example of the English, at the same time aspiring to greater things. Two Indian princes, one aspiring to be Nabob of the Carnatic, the other Subahdar of the Deccan, appealed to the French to aid them in enforcing by arms their claims. Dupleix at a glance saw

what advantage might accrue to him in such an undertaking.
A detachment of forces under command of M. d'Auteuil was
granted. They advanced upon the reigning prince (Anwar-
ad-dien) and put his army to flight, the prince being among
the slain. One of his sons was taken prisoner. The other
escaped with the army. This victory was not followed up by
the Indian forces. According to their custom they preferred
to enjoy some of the fruits of their success and make a display
of their power, for they already felt they were in possession
of their claims. After whiling away time in Arcot and Pondicherry, making display of their pomp and power, they proceeded against Tanjore; but the Rajah by skilfully conducting
the negotiations delayed the plans of his enemies until Nazir
Jung with a considerable force was approaching. This
caused them to hastily retreat to Pondicherry. Dupleix not
only gave them a large contingent but loaned them £50,000.
The English who had quite naturally looked with jealousy
and distrust upon the progress of the French now joined forces
with Nazir Jung. Mutiny broke out in the French ranks,
which so wrecked the hopes of M. d'Auteuil that he retreated
to Pondicherry, and the outlook for the confederates was anything but promising. Dupleix was reduced to great extremity,
yet his shrewdness helped him to extricate himself. Failing
to negotiate with Nazir, he opened correspondence with
some discontented officers in his army. He sent M. d'Auteuil,
who took the field again; this time with some success. The
English became disgusted with the inactivity of their allies
and withdrew from their support. Successes of the French
at length aroused Nazir from his voluptuous inactivity; but
he was too late. Dupleix, who had conducted all along his
negotiations with the Subahdar (Nazir) and the traitors, had
just agreed upon terms with the former, when his officers
receiving orders from the traitors marched upon Nazir, who
in the conflict was killed. One Mirzapha Jung was at once
made Subahdar. Dupleix was appointed governor of the
Mogul dominions on the Coromandel coast. The French
were now the great power in Southern India, their sway ex-

tending over a territory as large as France. Mirzapha was killed in a conflict with some of his rebellious forces as they were advancing into the interior of the Deccan. Bussy, the commanding officer of the French in attendance, at once released a brother of the late monarch and raised him to the throne. He, of course, owing all to the French, was ever ready to lend ear to their plans. The English at length, dreading the further extension of the French power, sent a contingent force to aid in the defense of Trichinopoly, the strongest position of their ally, Mohammed Ali, in the Carnatic. Another force was sent from Fort St. David, but neither distinguished itself by its military operations. Still other re-inforcements were sent, yet it seemed very doubtful if they would be able to hold out. The genius of Captain Clive now came to the rescue. He took Arcot, followed up his victory by taking possession of a number of important points, and then returned to Fort St. David.

This young officer was the son of an English country gentleman of moderate means. As a boy he was characterized by his daring and impetuosity. At the age of nineteen he was sent out to India as a writer.* In this capacity he was not very popular among the Company's servants. He was granted the privilege of entering the military service after Madras was taken by the French, and the first engagement in which he took part was at the siege of Pondicherry.

New troops were coming to the aid of Trichinopoly. Major Lawrence, who had now returned from England, moved forward at the head of 1,500 men, 400 of them Europeans. Mohammed Ali had by large promises been able to

* He landed in Madras, Thursday, May 31st, 1744, from steamer "Winchester," having been more than two years on the voyage, their letters from England being dated March 2nd, 1742. September following he drew his first quarter's pay £1 5s., his salary being £5 a year. In a letter from Court of Directors we find the following: "Be sure to encourage Ensign Clive in his martial pursuits according to his merit."—Madras Records, quoted by Wheeler.

engage the Prince of Mysore and a body of Mahrattas. This formidable force now compelled the French to retreat. Being overtaken, the natives deserting, the French surrendered themselves prisoners of war. The English were exultant, imagining the Carnatic already under their power. But Dupleix was persistent. The hostilities continued with varying results. The French at length succeeded in winning over to their side the Mahrattas and the Regent of Mysore. The siege of Trichinopoly was continued through a period of about eighteen months. The home governments attempted to settle the affairs of the Indian disputes. The question was whether or not Mohammed Ali, the friend of the English, should be recognised as Nabob of the Carnatic. The French opposing, all attempts to settle this question in India failed. A commission in London also had the same result. At length a new governor was sent out to supersede Dupleix, and with power to make terms with the English. In the meantime England had sent out some new troops which added so much to their strength that the French were no longer their equals. Dupleix returned to France. Terms were agreed upon which were in the main very favorable to the English. The recent acquisitions and achievements of Bussy which had "made the French masters of the sea-coast of Coromandel and Orixa in an uninterrupted line of 600 miles from Medapilly to the Pagoda of Jagernaut,"* " and which," says Wilks, " not only afforded the requisite pecuniary resources, but furnished the convenient means of receiving reinforcements of men and military stores from Pondicherry and Mauritius, and thus enabled Bussy to extend his political views to the indirect or absolute empire of Deccan on the south," were given up on the part of the French. Mohammed Ali was left the undisputed ruler of the Carnatic. This treaty being concluded, the French and English governors who had formulated it returned to England. But the expected peace did not come. There was scarce a lull in the hostilities. They

* Orme, Vol. I., p. 334, quoted by Mill.

continued until the declaration of war between France and England in 1756.

About this time affairs on the other side of India were assuming interesting proportions. The Mahratta power had extended over a great part of the Indian Continent. Each year they had assumed larger proportions. They made almost regularly annual incursions into the territories of their neighboring princes. The English at Calcutta had given offence to Suraja Dowla, Subahdar of Bengal. He marched upon Calcutta (June 18th, 1756). The Governor and a number of others, including the women, escaped to a boat and left those remaining in the fortifications to defend themselves as best they could. At length the place was taken. Casting about for a place to confine the prisoners, the native officers discovered the room used by the English for their prison. " It was unhappily a small, ill-aired, and unwholesome dungeon, called the Black Hole." In this dungeon the 146 unfortunate prisoners were thrust,—only 23 were taken out alive the next morning. The descriptions of that night as told by some of the survivors are almost too horrible to reproduce in print. To die from suffocation in such a small apartment must have been one of the worst forms of death. Clive had been to England, been made Lieutenant-Colonel and Deputy Governor of Fort St. David. Upon the disastrous news from Calcutta he proceeded to that point with a force from Madras. He obtained (Jan. 2nd, 1757) possession of Calcutta with little effort, and made terms with the Nabob. News of the declaration of war between the mother countries now reached India. Hostilities were begun against the French in Bengal. The Nabob was not pleased with this turn of affairs. Clive then joined some rebels in the Subahdar's camp in a plan to dethrone him, placing Meer Jaffier, who had been some time " pay-writer general " in the Subahdar's army, on the throne. The English took the field, but were only joined by Meer Jaffier in the midst of the battle of Plassy (June 23rd, 1757) which resulted in the complete success of the schemes of the confederates, Suraja Dowla being captured and put to death, and his successor ruled by the favor of the English.*

*In coming to terms with the rebels the English were not at all backward in their demands. For losses of Calcutta 10,000,000 rupees were demanded for the Company, 5,000,000 for the English inhabitants, 2,000,000 for the Indians and 7,000,000 for the Armenians; also that 2,500,000 should be given to the squadron and a like sum to the army. In addition to these extravagant demands, 1,280,000 rupees were demanded for the Governor, Clive, and the members of the Council. It was stipulated that the French should be forever shut out of Bengal, that an extent of territory adjacent to Calcutta should be held by the Company upon an annual payment of rents.—Mill, Vol. II., p. 113.

PART II.

CHAPTER I.

The Rise of Dominion.

One hundred and fifty years in India! Excepting possibly the dreams of Josiah Child and his brother, who, in 1684, was given the official title of Captain-General and Admiral of India, there had been no thought of dominion. To and from Madras, Bombay and Calcutta, they conducted their commercial enterprises. The East India Company had as its chief income the profits of its trading monopoly. It transmitted to its agencies in India and China effects to the value of scarce a million annually. By their domestic trade in India and their selling their effects at good profits both in the East and in England, the Company had a balance of about a million to defray expenses in Leadenhall Street, and to make their annual dividends. At each of their three important centers was stationed a Governor or President, and a Council, which managed the affairs of the district and the sub-agencies of their respective centers. The Company's resources were not indicative of what was so soon to follow. It was Dupleix, with his schemes so brilliant, so wide-sweeping, that first stirred the ambition in the breast of the Englishmen in India. And on no one were these impressions more powerful than upon young Clive. Dupleix had seen the disintegrating empire as it was. He knew its weaknesses. He knew the strength of a handful of his own countrymen well-armed, and knew equally well the power of money—or how to hold out the tempting bait of power to the native princes. His ambition pictured to him a great French empire with a king-maker at its head, drawing vast revenues, wielding vast power, and he saw himself as that great functionary. Had his company and his government backed him up to any considerable extent, had he been less vain, a little more courageous, things in India would to-day have presented an entirely different appearance. But with the departure of Dupleix from India the grand schemes of French dominion in the East vanished.

Young Clive had learned much in the few months he had been in conflict with the French. He saw all that Dupleix had seen. He had the daring of the French Governor, was more courageous, and had less of vanity. We cannot doubt but that Clive saw the possibilities which were before him in India. Yet he seems for some time to have taken the course he did more to make secure the Company's trade than toward securing any considerable extent of territory. But with the battle of Plassy (June 22nd, 1757), and the conditions of the treaty with Meer Jaffier we must date the Anglo-Indian Empire.

The first decade was not altogether auspicious to the English who had so successfully carried all before them. Some new French troops had been landed at Pondicherry. Then some months later Count Lally, who had been appointed Commander-in-chief of all the French forces in India, arrived with large re-inforcements. France was expecting great things from this general. Lally was anxious to fulfil their highest hopes. He had a force sufficient to drive the English out of India[*]—and so he meant to do. The English were

---

[*] Lord Clive himself said in his evidence before the committee in 1772: " Mr. Lally arrived with such force as threatened not only the destruction of all the settlements there, but of all the East India Company's possessions, and nothing saved Madras from sharing the fate of Fort St. David, at that time, but their want of money, which gave time for strengthening and reinforcing the place."—Quoted by Mill.

Lally was an Irishman devoted to James II. He had planned an invasion of England, had captured English officers, and had on many occasions shown his hatred. He was courageous, but over-ardent and

thrown into great alarm by the actions of their enemies. The French marched upon Fort St. David, and compelled its surrender. Devi-Cotah soon followed and Lally returned in triumph to Pondicherry. But he was not popular. He treated the officials as if they were all dishonest, and only looking to one end—the building up for themselves of great fortunes. He soon became embarassed for want of provisions. His unpopularity made it almost impossible to supply the deficiencies. From Fort St. David he had written to the Governor of Pondicherry : "This letter shall be an eternal secret between you, Sir, and me, if you afford me the means of accomplishing my intrigue. I left you 100,000 livres of my own money to aid you in providing the funds which it requires. I found not, upon my arrival, in your purse, and in that of your whole council, the resource of 100 pence. You, as well as they, have refused me the support of your credit. Yet, I imagine you are all of you more indebted to the Company than I am. If you continue to leave me in want of everything, and exposed to contend with universal disaffection, not only shall I inform the King and the Company of the warm zeal which their servants here display for their interest, but I shall take effectual measures for not depending, during the short stay I wish to make in this country, on the party spirit and the personal views with which I perceive that every member appears occupied, to the total hazard of the Company."* This accounts for his expedition against the King of Tanjore from whom he expected to extract great treasure. It resulted in nothing but disappointments. His laying siege to Madras failed, due to the arrival of the English fleet (1760).

With the retreat of the French from Madras the English on that side of India took courage. The next year (1761)

somewhat impetuous. Added to these characteristics his earlier successes had given him a touch of vanity and made him presumptuous. But war in Europe and in India had not much in common, as he soon learned.

* Memoire, Pièces Justificatives, p. 30, quoted by Mill.

they took Pondicherry. The French were made prisoners of war and Lally returned to France to suffer imprisonment and death at the hands of the country he had so long served, and French dominion in Hindostan was at an end.

In Bengal, Jaffier was unable to liquidate his extravagant obligations to the English. He was indolent, and given to voluptuous life. He had made great concessions to the English, ceding them the revenues of certain districts, granting them the monopoly of saltpetre and other valuable commercial privileges. He knew, however, that, as he had been raised to his position by the English, he could at any time be deposed by them, and he sought to make himself secure by allies. The Council at Calcutta at length determined to ask his resignation. After this event he retired to Calcutta and lived the life of a private gentleman.

His son-in-law, Meer Cassim, was made his successor. He showed considerable talent and vigor in a judicious management of affairs, succeeding in paying the arrears due to the English. Mutual jealousies soon arose. The English were carrying forward a system of extortions which almost ruined the country. These measures led to war. The English determined to depose Cassim. The struggle continued some time. New alliances were raised up against the English, but they made a brilliant campaign, gained no less than five important victories, reduced every stronghold that opposed them, making themselves masters of the great central plain of India. Clive, who had quitted India some time before, now (1765) returned as Commander-in-chief, President and Governor in Bengal. Upon his arrival in India, learning of the successful issue of the Company's measures in Bengal, he wrote: "We have at last arrived at that critical period which I have long foreseen: I mean that period which renders it necessary for us to determine whether we can or shall take the whole to ourselves. . . . Sujah Dowla is beat from his dominion; we are in possession of it, and it is scarcely hyperbole to say: to-morrow the whole Mogul Empire is in our power." Farther in the same letter he goes on to say: "Can it then be doubted that a large army of Europeans will effectually preserve us sovereigns, not only holding in awe the attempts of any country prince, but by rendering us so truly formidable that no French, Dutch, or other enemy, will presume to molest us." And again, "We must indeed become Nabobs ourselves, in fact if not in name;—perhaps totally so without disguise, but on this subject I cannot be certain until my arrival in Bengal."*

The keen perception of Clive had at once shown him the bent of things. From that time on England was to be a power—a nation in India. They were to make and unmake kings, or assume the power first hand for themselves. He had returned to India with high ideals of purging the Company's affairs of its many evils. He found "but anarchy, confusion, and, what is worse, an almost general corruption," and he at once took upon himself the " resolution of cleansing the Augean Stable." True, private trade had flourished in face of orders from the Company; bribes had been received ; presents of great value had been accepted by those who stood highest in authority.

Clive himself during his first stay in Bengal had not hesitated to accept most important favors from the native rulers. Men were constantly returning to England with vast fortunes, which they had hastily accumulated, and it must be remembered that this great wealth was somehow accumulated in one of the poorest (financially) countries of the time. The manner often of making a fortune in India would not reflect much credit upon the English people if known in detail. August 12th, 1765, less than a decade after the horrors of the Black Hole, Clive succeeds in winning for the English the legal possession under title of Indian law indisputable, an extent of territory larger in area than the whole of France. Calcutta, from that time, becomes the capital of Bengal. We shall find, although there were constant conflicts with the natives in different parts, there was little additional acquisition until some thirty years later, during the time of the Marquis of Wellesley.

* Quoted by Mill.

CHAPTER II.

ON THE WEST COAST.

WHILE Clive was laying the broad foundations of dominion in the north-east, Hyder Ali, a Mussulman of humblest birth, but gifted with shrewd daring and skill as a soldier, was raising upon the ruins of the broken members of the old Empire a dominion for himself. He was a man far above the average native prince. Combined with his military skill was a wonderful capacity as a ruler. He rose, as most native rulers rise, through military power. The depredations common among those people he reduced to a definite system. He had equipped himself largely by plunder, giving half to his army, retaining the other half for himself. He had distinguished himself in a conflict with the Mahrattas. He had at length made himself the ruler of a vast extent of country which made up the kingdom of Mysore. The other powers of southern India took alarm. Nizam Ali, Subahdar of the Deccan, and Madoo Rao, of the Mahrattas, formed a confederacy to check the growing power of Hyder. The English agreed to furnish an auxiliary force. In this first war between the English and the Mysore Prince one victory shed a momentary luster on the English forces. Colonel Smith, with an army of 1,500 Europeans and 9,000 Sepoys, defeated Hyder and his allies. The war ended, however, ingloriously and disastrously for the English by a peace in 1769, leaving affairs as they stood before the war. The result in London was deplorable. These wars and their outcome had reduced the price of Indian stock by 60 per cent. The Company was on the verge of hopeless insolvency. The affairs of the Company were largely laid to the charge of the Company's servants and to their constant war in India.

In 1769 (September 15th), the General Court of the Company appointed a commission to investigate Indian affairs, and gave them their instructions. After enjoining care for their property and harmony among its servants: "We desire you will consider and regard, as a most principal object, the restoring of peace in India upon a solid and permanent basis: but in pursuing the measures necessary to this end, we enjoin you to provide effectually for the honor and security of our faithful ally Mohamed Ally Cawn, Nabob of Arcot." This reads very much like a paradox; keep the peace and yet protect their ally, which meant make war. Again: "It may be prudent to make known to the Powers in India that it is by no means the intention of the Company to encroach upon their neighbors, or to acquire an extension of Dominion by Conquest, and that it is their determined resolution always to adhere to" treaties and limit themselves " to the revenues of Bengal and their present possessions."* About the same time the Governor of Fort St. George sent a Mr. Pybus to negotiate with the Nabob. In his consultations (January, 1768) we find the following: "The Nabob may be assured that we never shall make a peace with Hyder Ally unless reduced to it through necessity or superior force. He has given us too many proofs that he is too dangerous a neighbor to be left in the government of the Mysore country, and that, while he governs, we shall be obliged to keep up more forces to protect the Carnatic than the revenues of it will maintain," and they "resolved to obtain, if possible," from the Subahdar

---

* There are a number of interesting bits of information regarding this period in the records of the India Office. We learn that this committee consisted of Henry Van Sittart, Luke Scrafton, and Francis Forde. They were each to receive £1,000 per annum; were accompanied by a Secretary who was allowed £500, and a chaplain and surgeon were also in attendance.

From the same folio: "The procuring of raw silk for the manufactures of Great Britain is now become a great national object." The production of opium and raw silk is to receive every encouragement.

Again, showing their efforts to stop private trade, they gave orders that all persons in their service who were engaged in a monopoly in cotton goods or other articles were to be dismissed from the service.—Records in India Office (1769).

and the Mogul privileges placing the "country on same footing as the Provinces in Bengal have lately been put, and the Nabob or one of his family shall actually be intrusted with the management of affairs on behalf of the Company, so that both countries may enjoy peace, so far as regards each other."* The Company were often given to so wording their instructions that their servants might be justified in following more than one interpretation. The year 1770 was marked by one of those famines which so often leave destitute the Indian provinces. It was estimated that almost one-third of the population of Bengal perished. The Company's affairs grew from bad to worse. They implored, after securing loans from the bank, a million pounds from the public to help them out of present difficulties. This stirred deep feeling in England against the Company. Its managers, officers, and servants were accused of mismanagement. The enormous fortunes of private individuals which were accumulated during the famine by those who were in the Company's service contrasted strangely with the present state of its treasury. James, writing recently, says there are men living in England to-day who were taught as children to " shudder at the crimes of the Englishmen, who had made enormous fortunes by the starvation of millions of their fellow-creatures " in India. Men did not stop to consider the laws of supply and demand. While much wealth was unjustly accumulated, we must grant that most of the more serious charges were without proper foundation. It is well-known that Lord Clive, in the face of all his services to the Company, did not escape censure.

The House of Commons passed the following resolution : " That acquisitions made by the armes of the State belong to the State alone, and that it is illegal in the servants of the State to appropriate such acquisitions to themselves. That this rule has been systematically violated by the English functionaries in Bengal." This was an indirect censure of the action of Clive, who had accepted the revenues of a certain

* Records.

Indian territory, conferred on him by Meer Jaffier. The House of Commons was right in not passing the actual vote of censure, which it would have been impossible justly to follow by any confiscation of Clive's property. What had been done in the East had been done by him as servant of the Company at their expense and risk. The Crown had given up to the Company the profits of their territorial acquisitions, and all the spoils of war. The breach of trust was condoned, as also were the perquisites which their agent had taken for himself while gaining an empire for them; and after the acts complained of, they had invoked his aid to save them from ruin. But the resolution and the discussions in Parliament were there for the future as a warning of the stern relentlessness with which the English people would view oppression stained with personal corruption, and that far off as India was the stories of wrongs done there might easily raise the terrible wrath of an English House of Commons. Not content with mere monitory resolutions, the legislation enacted in express terms, " that it should be a misdemeanor for an officer in the East to accept any present under any pretence from any native, prince or person." In 1773 there was an act passed by the House of Commons for regulating Indian affairs. This marks a real commencement of what we may call British rule in India. They thus begin to assume some actual responsibility for vast territories won by the servants of a trading monopoly.

CHAPTER III.

Parliament Begins to Assume some Authority in Indian Affairs.

The Supreme Government was vested in a Governor-General and Council of four members located at Calcutta. The other Presidencies were subject to the Bengal Council in all questions relating to peace and war, otherwise the investiture of the powers of the Governor-General and Council did not materially affect the old system. Their power of legislation was subject to the control of the Supreme Court of Judicature. The chief function of this departure was, however, to supply the powers of criminal jurisdiction which had before been entirely in the hands of the Company. It thus represented the paramount authority of the Sovereign.*

In London by the new arrangement, practically speaking, a Director was one for life. There were to be twenty-four, one-fourth going out every year, the vacancies to be supplied by new men; but as retiring members were eligible for re-election it simply meant thirty Directors with one-fifth all the time taking a vacation. So true was the practical working of this system that the case of a Director not holding office for life became the exception. "And the Home Government became a sort of aristocracy—a life peerage."†

---

* "The defect in the institution seemed to be this: that no rule was laid down, either in the act or the charter, by which the Court was to judge. . . . Provision was made for the administration of justice in the remotest part of Hindostan; as if it were a province in Great Britain. Your Committee have long had the constitution and conduct of this Court before them and they have as yet been able to discover very few instances of relief given to the natives against the corruptions or oppressions of British subjects in power. . . . The Court has been generally terrible to the natives, and has distracted the government of the Company."—Mr. Burke in the Ninth Report of Select Committee, 1783, quoted by Mill.

† Sir W. M. James, "British in India."

And yet such a Government was not so objectionable as it might appear on the surface. The shareholders were largely the wealthy business men, merchants and bankers, or Anglo-Indians, of London. Through their experience and training they were eminently qualified to make a good election. They must look to the best management, for mismanagement could not be to their advantage. They had every inducement to re-elect those men most fitted for the control of their affairs. A wrong choice of officials might mean a loss of their possessions as well as their fortunes.

The Directors each had the right to nominate a young man to be a writer in their Indian service. But once in India his rise must depend almost entirely upon his own merits. His patron Director had nothing more to do with him, and unless he drew attention by some worthy acts he was in all probability completely forgotten. By successive steps, showing the proper capacity, the way was open to the highest positions in their service. We have seen how Clive rose from writer to founder of the Empire. We shall presently see how another young servant came to be the first Governor-General in India.

The seats in the Council were of course only open to those who distinguished themselves in the Company's service. The Company's servants were largely drawn from the old Scotch families, "a race as yet unrivalled in the qualities and arts by which poor adventures win wealth and position abroad." It required no little courage to leave the old home, with its memories, and ship to tropical seas, where there was so little to attract save a fairly good salary, or opportunity to win private fortunes, or a great name through military service.

Yet " the highest qualities of soldier, administrator and diplomatist" were in demand, and the reward of such qualities was sure. And it has been true of India, as it has of almost every country, the times and their needs produce the proper qualities in some leader, who rises fully developed for his work.

After the law passed in England making it illegal for those in the Company's service to accept bribes, the affairs of the Company present a more attractive appearance, although the practice was probably never quite put down.

The great weakness was that India was poor. She could ill afford to bear the expenses of an English army when the expense of one private soldier cost the earnings of not less than forty native laborers, and one of the higher officials annually consumed the equivalent of the earnings of some two thousand natives. At the time of which we now speak India was but a barbarous country. There were not yet those accompaniments of civilization such as public highways, code of laws, or municipal organization. Bengal yielded comparatively a small revenue.

CHAPTER IV.

WARREN HASTINGS.

AMONG the passengers on an Indian steamer, leaving London in mid-winter, 1750, was a youth of seventeen. He was bright and promising. But left an orphan in early childhood, losing later his nearer relatives, those who had him in charge shipped him off to India, where he would give least trouble to them. He was placed at a desk in the Secretary's office in Calcutta, and afterwards was assigned similar duties in the Company's offices in Cossimbazar. It was during the difficulties with Suraja Dowla that Warren Hastings gave promise of what he might become. Clive had recognized the ability of this young clerk and appointed him to an important position.

In 1761 he became a member of the Council at Calcutta. After a four years' stay in England (1764-68) he returned to India, and gradually rose in the estimation of the Directors until he was honored in 1773 in the " Regulating Act " by being made first Governor-General in India. No other man in their employ was better fitted for such an important post. He was gifted with exceptional powers of organization and control.

Clive had laid the territorial foundation of a British empire in Bengal.

Hastings created a British administration for the territory Clive had won. He established direct rule over Bengal. The Nabob became a pensionary in the Company. A system was formulated for all of Bengal. No one man is more conspicuous in the history of the British in India. But he belongs largely to the personal biography and to British oratory and literature probably more than to the growth of power in India. He found and left the Anglo-Indian Empire little changed as to its boundaries. He did enlarge the territories to a certain extent and greatly consolidated the whole, but his chief work was in the progress he made in the internal organization. For the first time within half a century Bengal was under the sway of a power strong enough to protect its people.

Hastings had to carry forward his work under great difficulties. He was constantly living under pressure on the part of his superiors, such as only the highest virtue could have withstood. While the Directors of the Company never applauded a crime, yet they were constantly demanding money. "Govern leniently and send more money; practise strict justice and moderation towards neighboring powers, and send more money." * Says Macaulay: "This is, in truth, the sum of almost all the instruction that Hastings ever received from home. Now these instructions being interpreted mean simply, ' Be the father and oppressor of the people; be just and unjust, moderate and rapacious '."

Although not over scrupulous himself, he put down corruption among the Company's servants. He was able to raise the revenues of Bengal without losing the respect of the natives. He sent to the Directors large sums of money. He kept in touch with the people, knew their language, understood their natures, could sympathize with their plans.

The Mahrattas were becoming a great power in India. It looked as if they might succeed largely to the position of the old Moguls. Hastings recognized the danger. England was coming to a conflict with her colonies across the Atlantic. She seemed beset on every hand. "Great as were the faults of Hastings it was happy for our country that at that juncture, the most terrible through which she has ever passed, he was ruler of her Indian dominions." † He succeeded in so managing affairs that in India the English lost nothing, although losers in almost every other part of their possessions.

---

* Macaulay's " Warren Hastings."
† Macaulay's " Warren Hastings."

Hastings maintained his position during the serious troubles with great courage. He met the attempts of the Mahrattas, extricated himself from the most intricate and dangerous positions with skill.

While beating back the Mahrattas, Hyder decides to make a second attempt against the English. He, too, had been compelled to wage war against the Mahrattas, and had expected the English to aid him in defending his possessions. Their neglect roused his anger. France promises to combine with him against the English. He proceeds against Madras (1780). Flames and smoke warn the inhabitants of his approach. He defeats the forces sent against him. In less than one month from the beginning of the war, the affairs of the English seem on the verge of ruin on that side of India. News is brought to Hastings. He patches up a treaty with his northern foes and sends his troops under the command of General Eyre Coote; for with Hyder this is a struggle of life and death. At length affairs take a more favorable turn. At Novo Porto * the English redeem themselves. The conflict however continues. In 1782 Hyder dies. The command is taken up by his son Tippoo. Then followed during the next year peace between the English and French. Not until 1784 were the English able to come to terms with Tippoo. Having brought difficulties to a favorable conclusion, Hastings prepared to follow his wife, who on account of ill health had preceded him, to England.

He had saved the English possessions in the East—all that Clive had won he had preserved. Defective as must have been the affairs due to the wars and the large sums of money which the Governor-General was compelled to raise, it is probable that within the memory of the oldest man Bengal had not enjoyed such a season of equal security and

---

* "The consequences of this victory were highly important. Hyder abandoned his designs upon the southern provinces. Tippoo raised the siege of Wandewash, and both retired with the whole of their army to the neighbourhood of Arcot."—Mill, Vol. II. Book II., p. 585.

prosperity. Hastings left India amid the most gratifying marks of favor, not only from his countrymen but from natives as well. He hoped for great rewards upon his return to England. His rule had been characterized by foresight, courage and wisdom. But in zealously serving his masters he had overstepped the bounds of the English conscience. Charges were preferred against him, which were continued through seven long years, leaving him acquitted indeed, but a ruined man. He spent the remainder of his years in private life, dying in 1818, eighty-six years of age, and thirty-four years after he had landed in England, expecting "a coronet, a red riband, a seat at the Council Board, an office in Whitehall." But all his hopes were blasted. Indian Governors learned that English people, so widely separated from India, could arouse themselves to a high degree of sympathy for their subjects in the tropics.

"Clive notwithstanding his brilliant deeds, and after his second administration so great and good, scarcely escaped a Parliamentary censure for his early corrupt malversion in office.

Hastings narrowly escaped a conviction for the oppression, exaction, and cruelty which stained an administration so successful and so popular."—James.

CHAPTER V.

UP TO THE END.

THE events of the past few years had directed public attention in England towards Indian affairs. Actions against Clive and Hastings, especially the latter, were events of great moment among British statesmen. They began to feel some personal responsibility for the government of their subjects in India. This found expression in Mr. Pitt's Indian Bill (passed 1784).

By this Bill the chief power was vested in a Board of Control "with a superintendence and control over all the British territorial possessions in India and over the affairs of the Company in England." The power virtually was taken from the Court of Directors and given over to a Secret Committee, consisting of three members. Nothing could be done without the sanction of the Board of Control, which, although it was to consist of six members, became in fact vested in "The President of the Board of Commissioners for the affairs of India"—legally named, James says. No despatch could be sent out without his sanction. He could alter or reverse any measure framed by the Directors, and they must submit to his alterations. He could demand a despatch at will from the Court of Directors, and they must formulate it according to his pleasure.

The higher political matters were given over to the Secret Committee, which alone communicated with the Board of Control.

Another measure included in Pitt's Bill was that every employee returning from India should give an inventory of the property which he brought back with him.

A few acts, such as the appointment of the Governor-

General, Commander-in-chief, and other selections for the highest offices required the authority of the Board of Control and the Secret Committee, each having the power of recall. It was a curious arrangement, "the most singular scheme of government perhaps ever devised".* How it worked is a marvel. But it was successful much more than would seem possible. We must bear in mind also that in India at the different Presidencies the plan of government was even more intricate. There were millions of subjects to govern and few governors, but withal the machinery of government moved along with some sort of progressive regularity.

Lord Cornwallis landed in Calcutta, September, 1786, as the second Governor-General, and the first who united to his office that of Commander-in-chief of the army. He had borne a prominent part in the war of the American Revolution. He was considered one of England's ablest generals. The Company were firm in their desire for peace, and Cornwallis came out, full of great plans. He would right the injustice, do away with oppression and fraud, make India a real nation and govern it, not like Hastings, more after the Indian's policy, but on a plan modelled on the home government. But he proposed in vain. It was for him to embark in an arduous war, make large additions of dominion and combine a system of alliances more sweeping than any yet made.

In 1789 Tippoo of Mysore gave offence to the English, and the third Mysore war followed. The Company was ill-prepared for war with this powerful Prince. He had made use of all the European engineers he could induce to enter his service, and had everywhere strengthened his country. He was cruel, ambitious and faithless; a fanatic in religion, compelling his subjects to embrace Mohammedanism. He treated his prisoners in a way which showed the untamable passion and great ferocity of his nature. The struggle continued for nearly three years before it was brought to a successful issue. Tippoo was at length driven into his

* James.

capital, Seringapatam, but was unable to long hold out against the British forces. March 19th, 1792, he accepted the terms proposed by the besiegers. This treaty compelled him to cede one-half of his territories to the English and their allies; to pay nearly three and a half millions sterling for the expenses of the war; to restore all prisoners of war, and deliver his two sons, ages eight and ten years, to Cornwallis as hostages.

After the war Cornwallis turned his attention to the " Permanent Settlement " of the revenue. He carried out measures of government which will cause his name to be remembered in India long after he is forgotten as a military man.* As we have seen there was then little government in India as we now think of that term, and Cornwallis was chiefly selected to carry forward and institute some reforms in administration. In 1793 (Sept.) he resigned, thinking probably as did Hastings, that he was leaving India quiet, the country favored with settled peace. But the time was not yet ripe for the fulfilment of such expectations.

Sir John Shore was the third Governor-General. During his administration, which was largely a peaceful one, much encouragement was given to missionaries. But the Anglo-Indian Empire was not left by him in a stronger position. His successor, the Earl of Mornington,† afterward Marquis of Wellesley, was enjoined by the Company to continue a peaceful policy; to wage no war against a native power, nor to add a single square mile to the Company's territory; but circumstances ruled otherwise. He found India in a very critical condition.

The Mysore chief had been preparing himself for another struggle against the English. His hatred against them was intense. Word was brought to the Governor-General that a proclamation had been issued by the Governor-General of

---

* " If the foundations of the system of civil administration were by Hastings, the superstructure was raised by Cornwallis."—Hunter's Gazetteer of India, p. 392.

† He was an elder brother of the Duke of Wellington.

Mauritius (French), referring to Tippoo : " This prince desires to form an offensive and defensive alliance with the French. He promises to furnish everything necessary. He declares that he has made every preparation to receive the succours which may be sent to him. In a word, he only waits the moment when the French shall come to his assistance to declare war against the English, whom he ardently desires to expel from India. As it is impossible for us to reduce the number of soldiers of the 107th and 108th regiments, and of the regular guard, we invite the citizens who may be disposed to enter as volunteers to enrol themselves and to serve under the banners of Tippoo. The Prince desires to be assisted by the free citizens of color; we therefore invite all who are willing to serve, to enrol themselves." This had but a small following, and " Citizen Tippoo," as some of his republican French adherents addressed him, had built his hopes upon feeble foundations.

Wellesley at once took active measures.* Within two months from the time of the opening of the campaign,† Seringapatam was taken and Tippoo found among the dead. The Empire of the House of Hyder had suddenly been subverted. It had risen and assumed its mighty proportions, "a baseless fabric of vision." It had had little foundation. This favorable conclusion of the Mysore difficulties drew upon Wellesley the enthusiastic applause of his countrymen and congratulations poured in on him from every quarter. It was the finishing stroke against the enemies of the English on that side of India. From that time peace has hovered over Madras and the Carnatic.

This conflict was soon followed by another with the Mahrattas. Lord Wellesley seems to have had two plans firmly fixed in his mind. One the necessity of getting a hold

---

* Speaking of this year James says : " In fine there never was a war begun with more just cause, or a plainer necessity, or more exceptionally conducted, or the prizes of which were more legitimately acquired."

† In this campaign the Duke of Wellington began his military career.

on the ever-increasing power of the Mahrattas, and the other the necessity of excluding the French from all the native powers. The exclusion of the French meant nothing more nor less than that the English should control the whole of the sea-coast. The Mahratta power had grown until its territories were extensive. In its relation to India it may be compared, as to extent of territory, with the relation of the old German Empire to the rest of Europe. The right sort of a prince could in all probability amalgamate the whole under one ruler, and thus make his kingdom most formidable.

The war against the Mahrattas had proven highly successful. By the treaty in 1803 vast territories were added to the English dominions. The whole sea-coast was now either in their hands or under the control of their allies. The French in India were annihilated. The English were the dictatorial power of India.

Wellesley was very sanguine over the reign of peace which he now believed he had inaugurated on the Indian Continent. During the remainder of his stay he devoted himself to the carrying forward of immense improvements.*

In 1805 this official who had accomplished so much returned to England. He left his country a greater power in India than the Mohammedan rulers had ever been. The Anglo-Indian Empire was on a firm footing. He increased the revenues from seven and one-fourth millions until in 1807 they amounted to thirteen and one-half millions. But the Indian debt had been at the same time increased. Englishmen at home read with alarm of an Indian debt of eleven millions.

Wellesley was generally on bad terms with the Directors who had been continually insisting upon pacific measures. He was aristocratic, imperious, but must be ranked with India's greatest rulers.

Renewed troubles were brewing with the Mahrattas

* Lord Wellesley had abolished sacrificing of children by throwing them to the alligators in the Ganges, in 1802.

before he departed from India. The fermentation continued, now and then breaking out in open hostilities. In finances one deficit follows another. The policy was peace, and peace at almost any sacrifice. But such a plan was not the one to pursue with Indian princes. The Company sighed for its old dividends. They even expressed the sentiment that they would gladly give up their territorial possessions to once again enjoy their trade monopoly uninterrupted.

In 1813 an act of great importance took place in the history of the Company. The outcry against the exclusive monopoly could no longer be withstood. This year the first great inroad in their exclusive privileges was made. The trade of the Company except to China was thrown open. China was left to them to enable the Company to pay its annual dividends of £600,000 a year, and to help defray territorial expenses. The same year the Marquis of Hastings arrived in India and assumed the responsibilities of the office of Governor-General. He found India's political horizon thick with clouds. Almost from his arrival he had to devote himself to the carrying forward of measures against various enemies. He pacified the Burmese, waged war with Nepaul, and after a long hard struggle humbled the Pindarrees. The treaties of November, 1817, and December, 1818, show the willingness of the Indian princes to submit to the authority of the English. The policy of Hastings was to claim paramount authority over the whole peninsula. He found India beset by every sort of difficulty upon his arrival in 1813. During the nine years of his administration he completed and consolidated " the edifice of empire which had been erected by Lord Wellesley on the foundations laid by Lord Clive."

Yet was India not to be blessed by any long period of peace. Lord Amherst succeeded the Marquis of Hastings, August, 1823. The principal event of his administration was the storming of Bhurtpore in the interior of India. Outside their territories a trouble arose which brought on a war with the Burmese which lasted almost two years. The contest ended successfully for the English, resulting in a considerable extension of territory in that direction. The policy of the Indian rulers was to resent every insult for the sake of prestige, while that of the Directors in London was ever for peace.

Lord William Bentinck, who was the successor (1827) of Amherst, ruled with singular moderation however. His only ambition was the promoting of the welfare of his Indian subjects. No general conflict took place during his administration, but some disturbances were agitating the borders of the Empire. During his term the abominable custom of burning widows of Hindoos with their husbands was made illegal and punishable in the criminal courts. There were also some additions made to the English possessions.

The charter of the Company had been granted from time to time for periods of twenty years, and each renewal had given occasion for national investigation into Indian affairs. With the Act of 1833 the Company's monopoly of the trade to China was taken from them. The exports from India were according to Hunter £9,674,000, and the imports £2,576,000. The official positions in India were at the same time thrown open to natives, irrespective of caste, creed or race. A number of new reforms were at the same time introduced in the Government. The law forbidding all British born subjects taking up residence in India without the Company's license (unless they were the Company's servants) was not repealed until 1833.

In 1839 there was a dread of Russian aggrandizement. All the European population of India was wrought up over it. It almost amounted to a monomania. There were all sorts of rumors filling the air. It was feared Afghans, Persians and Russians would combine and wipe out forever all the Englishman had won in the Orient. In such a course Russia would only have been following Turks, Afghans, and Aryans.

The great conflict with the Afghans followed. At the conclusion of this war Lord Auckland was succeeded by Lord Ellenborough.

The year 1842 closed both in India and England with great rejoicings and feelings of satisfaction. They felt that

G

the Eastern troubles were settled. The English had met such a succession of disasters as they had scarcely experienced in their history in the East.

Not only defeat but flight and dishonor had disgraced the English flag in India, and men had prophesied the overthrow of all their possessions.

Then followed the war in Sindh. Sir Charles Napier assumed command in Sindh. It was thought the success of the English arms in other quarters would bring these people to terms. It soon came to open hostilities, however, and continued with varying results during the administration of Lord Ellenborough. Peace never hovered long over India during the making of the Empire. In 1845 the first Sikh war broke out. It culminated in the battle of Aliwal and Sobraon, leaving the English masters of the Punjab.

This occurred during the administration of Lord Hardinge. He ruled with considerable wisdom. He encouraged general education, prohibited Sunday labor, opened the public service, under certain restrictions, to the native youths. Private enterprise sprung up, commencement was made toward introducing railways, etc. The year 1847 was comparatively quiet, and upon Lord Hardinge's departure from India, he was called "the pacific warrior, the happy statesman; the man who, in reality, brought peace to Asia."*

Lord Dalhousie in 1848 was the next Governor-General. He, as were almost invariably his predecessors, was soon involved in war. Sir W. Hunter, speaking of this Governor, says: "Lord Dalhousie completed the fabric of British rule in India."

An outbreak occurred at Multon which at length led to the second Sikh war. In 1840 (March 30th) a proclamation was issued declaring the Punjab under British control,† and measures carried out enforcing the proclamation.

* See *Calcutta Review*.

† "The Annexation of the Punjab and Burma are the crowning events of the 19th century."—Wheeler's "British India."

Lord Dalhousie followed ably his predecessor. Industries were encouraged. Railroads were largely extended. Telegraph lines were introduced. Cheap postage was inaugurated, and many reforms in the condition of trade were carried out. An Act was passed establishing trial by jury throughout British India. A School of Art was established, arrangements carried into effect for female education. In 1854 an Education Department was established. Steps were taken looking to a systematic extension of irrigation in India.

In 1852 the second Burmese war broke out, which resulted in the British territories being extended to include Rangoon and a great part of the province of Pegu.

By order of the Court of Directors one of the last acts of Dalhousie was the annexation of Oudh (1856). In 1854 the Governorship of Bengal, which had always been held by the Governor-General, was separated and given over to another official, known as the " Lieutenant-Governor of Bengal."

The Company's charter was renewed for the last time in 1853. No definite period was stipulated. It was to be forfeited at the pleasure of Parliament. The number of the Directors was reduced.

In 1856 Lord Canning became Governor-General, and was soon embarked in a war with Persia. This was followed in 1857 by that great uprising which shook the very foundations of British power, the Sepoy mutiny.

The regular army in India was now about 200,000. The Sepoys had for a century been the pride of the East India Company. They had taken an active part in the battle of Plassy, and had constantly grown more efficient. They were largely the instruments of the building up of the Empire. The difficulty arose from acts on the part of their superiors, who took steps which interfered with their religious customs.

The uprising was general. Fortunately it was put down and ended in a firmer consolidation of the English dominion.

In 1858 the East India Company ceased to exist. By Act of Parliament its government of India was handed over to the Crown. The Queen was formally proclaimed sovereign of India, and the Governor-General became her viceroy. A commercial company with its Court of Directors, dating from the time of the Tudors, passed away, but it had given birth to an empire which forms probably the brightest gem in the crown of the English Queen. England is an Asiatic power, wielding great power in the Orient. The English tongue encircles the world, and yet who can say we are even at the beginning of the end.

APPENDIX.

THERE were a number of important battles fought during the struggles for the conquest of Mysore ; the Mahratta country ; the Afghan war ; the Punjab conquests, etc. One may trace the growth of the Empire in these battles and their results. We have preferred, however, not to go into detail, but to take a somewhat different vantage ground. We have had enough of wars, and history is too often traced by streams of blood. We should be able to trace progress without using the dead bodies of our fellow men as the stepping stones.

For a full account of that disastrous retreat (January 6th, 1842) of the English forces from the Afghan country to Jellalabad, in which the whole force of nearly 16,500 people perished, we may refer the reader to Lady Sale's Diary, which gives a vivid description of that event which in its sad results is almost without a parallel.

CHARTERS OF EAST INDIA COMPANY.

I. 1600, Queen Elizabeth, December 31st, 1600-15.
II. 1609, James I., "perpetual."
III. 1657, Oliver Cromwell, giving exclusive rights to the United Company.
IV. 1661, Charles II., perpetual.
V. 1677, Charles II., perpetual.
VI. 1683, Charles II., perpetual.
VII. 1693, William III. and Mary, perpetual.
VIII. 1698-99, Anne, to 1726 nominally, actually to 1736.*

GOVERNORS AND GOVERNOR-GENERALS OF INDIA UNDER EAST INDIA COMPANY, 1758-1858.

1758. Lord Clive, Governor.
1760. Mr. Z. Holwell (*pro tem.*).
1760. Mr. Vansittart.
1765. Lord Clive.

* This made Old and English Companies the New Company.—Report on Old Records India Office, Sir George Birdwood, 1890.

1767. Mr. Harry Verelst.
1769. Mr. John Cartier.
1772. Mr. Warren Hastings. (First Governor-General).
1785. Sir John Macpherson (*pro tem.*).
1786. Marquis of Cornwallis.
1793. Sir John Shore. (Lord Teignmouth).
1798. Marquis of Wellesley.
1805. Marquis of Cornwallis.
1805. Sir George Barlow (*pro tem.*).
1807. Earl of Minto.
1813. Marquis of Hastings.
1823. Mr. John Adam (*pro tem.*).
1823. Lord Amherst.
1828. Mr. Butterworth Bayley (*pro tem.*).
1828. Lord William Cavendish Bentinck.
1835. Sir Charles Metcalf (*pro tem.*).
1836. Earl of Auckland.
1842. Earl of Ellenborough.
1844. Viscount Hardinge.
1848. Earl of Dalhousie.
1856. Earl Canning.

PRINCIPAL ACQUISITIONS OF TERRITORY IN INDIA.*

1639. Madraspatam.
1669. Bombay.
1690. Fort St. David.
1694. Anjengo.
1698. Calcutta.
1708. Tellicherry and Ennor.
1734. Dharmapatam Island.
1742. Villages in Chingleput.
1749. St. Thomé, Devikota and villages.
1750. Punnamali District.
1756. Villages in Kolaba and Ratnagiri Collectorates.
1757. 24 Parganahs.
1758. Vizagapatam.
1759. Nizampatam, Masulipatam, and towns in Godavari and Kishna Districts.
1760. Burdwan, Midnapore, Chittagong and Hill tracts of Chittagong.
1765. Bengal, Behar, Orissa, and Garo Hills.

1768. Circars in Ganjam, Vizagapatam, Godovari and Kistna Districts.
1772. Chunar and Allahabad Forts.
1775. Benares, Jaunpore, Mirzapore, and islands of Salsette and Karanjah.
1778. Nagore.
1781. Sadras, Bimlapatam, Palicole, Porto Novo Factory, Tuticorin, Negapatam.
1783. Porto Novo, Cuddalore.
1792. Calicut and parts of Malabar, Madura, Salem and North Arcot Districts.
1799. North Canara, South Canara, Coimbatore, Nilgiri Hills, Tanjore, and parts of Salem and North Arcot.
1800. The Ceded Districts (Madras Presidency), City Fort of Surat, etc.
1801. Etah, Etawah, Mainpuri, Fatehpore, Cawnpore, Allahabad, and other Districts of the North-West Provinces, Armagon, the Chingleput District, and Carnatic Payen Ghat.
1802. Other parts of Districts, North-West Provinces, and Parganas, in Ahmedabad, Kaira, Broach, and Surat Collectorates.
1803. Upper Doab, Banda, Hamirpur, Cuttack, Balasore, Broach, Hurriana, etc.
1805. Kaira and Karnal.
1810. Fatehabad.
1812. Ratnagiri Collectorate.
1814. Cochin.
1815. Parts of Simla District, Kumaon, Dehra Dun, etc.
1817. Saugor Districts, and parts of Ahmedabad, Kaira, Broach, Surat, and Thana Collectorates.
1818. Districts in Central Provinces, Ajmir, and parts of Poona, Ahmednagar, Sholapur, Sattara, Nasik, Khandesh, Kolaba, Ratnagiri, Dharwar, Belgaum, and Khaladghi Collectorates.
1818. Sirsa.
1822. Parts of Ahmednagar and Sholapur Collectorates.
1824. Pulicat, Chinsurah, Dacca, Patna.
1825. Assam, Naga Hills.
1826. Parts of Arakan and Tenasserim Divisions.
1829. Parts of Jaintia and Khasi Hills District.
1830. Cachar, Simla.

1834. Coorg.
1835. Jaintia, Darjeeling, Ferozepore, parts of Muzaffanagar, Mirat, Bulundshahr, Alighar, Katkhai and Katgurh.
1839. The Mandai State.
1840. Jalaun District and Banki.
1841. Assam Duars.
1843. Sind.
1844. Kolaba State.
1845. Tranquebar.
1846. Lahore and other parts of the Punjab.
1847. Parts of the Punjab.
1848. Parts of Sholapur, Satara, Dharwar, Belgaum, and Kaladgi Collectorates.
1849. Parts of the Punjab.
1850. Sambalpur, Sikhim, Sanawar.
1852. Oodeyput.
1854. Jhansi, Nagpur, Sanawar.
1856. Oudh, Tanjore Fort.
1857. Jhajjar Territory.
1858. Banpur and Shahgarh.
1860. Upper Godovari Districts, Nimar, Harda and Hindia.
1861. Panch Mahals, Shillong.
1865. Eastern Duars, Dewangiri, and Bengal Duars.
1878. The Peint State.
1886. Upper Burma.

* From "India Office Records" by Mr. F. C. Danvers.

―――――o―――――

VITA.

Ich bin den 3ten October 1863 geboren, als Sohn von William Thomas Cuppy und Martha Ann Cuppy, geborene Marts. Bis zu meinem siebzehntem Jahre habe ich blos Gelegenheit gehabt die Dorfschule zu besuchen. Im Jahre 1880 bin ich in das Gymnasium (High School) zu Rockville, Indiana, eingetreten. Ich vollendete den vierjährigen Kursus in drei Jahren. Im Herbst desselben Jahres wurde ich auf der Universität zu Franklin, Indiana, immatriculiert und am Ende des Sommersemesters 1888 hat die Universität mir das Baccalaureat verliehen. Sodann ging ich im Herbst 1889 nach England, wo ich zwei Semester auf der Universität Oxford studierte. Im Jahre 1891 kam ich nach Heidelberg. Daselbst habe ich besonders die Vorlesungen von Professor Erdmannsdörffer und Professor Ihne gehört. Daneben habe ich mich mit den hauptsächlichsten Geschichtswerken des Mittelalters und der Neuzeit beschäftigt.

H. A. CUPPY.

www.ingramcontent.com/pod-product-compliance
Lightning Source LLC
Chambersburg PA
CBHW020153170426
43199CB00010B/1013